TO THE PEOPLE WH
OUR LE

This book is dedicated to my academic colleagues, the staff, and the students at City University of Seattle in Vancouver, BC, Canada. Without their support and encouragement I would not have had the immense opportunity to engage in designing, developing, musing about, and implementing that which humanizes educational environments.

Particular mention goes to Dr. Arden Henley, Principal of Canadian Programs at City University of Seattle in Vancouver, who has an uncanny ability to notice what a person is passionate about and skilful with, and find a way to match that up with what is needed. As well, Colin Sanders, Director of Canadian Counselling Programs, whom I have known for several decades, and who likes to tell the story about how I hired *him* at an early point in both our careers, has provided me great support in my position as coordinator for the full-time Master of Counselling program. Everything I have written about is being enacted in this program.

Finally, a special mention to the students in full-time cohorts 2, 3, 4, and 5 with whom I have worked most closely in the last three and a half years. Their feedback indicates to me that they have learned and enjoyed the experience about as much as I have.

Avraham Cohen

To the cosmos that has inspired me to take my learning journey through hard times, good times, interesting times, painful times, and joyful times. To my mother who was a supreme master of survival and resilience, who instilled in me a primordial confidence. To my father who, even though shadowed with his own suffering, unconditionally trusted me to be well and do well. And to my two daughters, Lumina and Serenna, who have been teaching me ever since their birth that learning is all about unlearning, re-learning, and at times forgetting about learning and just playing. And to Avraham, my husband, who seems to have been appointed by my mother, as she was expiring with her last breath, to continue to teach me the most important lessons in life: the courage of unconditional love, humility, and kindness.

Heesoon Bai

All my life I have been a learner, a sojourner in the world of words. I am grateful for Kerry and Russell Leggo who often seemed befuddled by their son's passion for books, but bought them anyway and built bookcases to hold them. And I am grateful for Lana Verge who has walked beside me with abiding love for over forty years, patiently convinced that I was responding to an ineffable but evocative call. And I am grateful for Anna Reithmeier and Aaron Leggo who learned about the geography of Canada by driving back and forth across the country with their father behind the steering wheel, occasionally looking back, but mostly staring ahead into the rain, wind, sun, and snow, always hopeful. And I am grateful for Madeleine and Mirabelle Reithmeier, and Gwenoviere and Alexandria Leggo, who remind their grandfather daily that words cast spells full of the world's wonders.

Carl Leggo

To my parents, Jean and Buster Browne, who fanned the flames of learning in a little girl who took everything on with a passion. Their support was both tangible (all those wonderful books!) and intangible. They modelled curiosity, dedication, and strength. My father eschewed his actual first name, John, and was always known by his nickname. From him I learned to be true to myself. I am so grateful to Merv who took over when we married. He is always there—supportive, humorous, and insightful—giving me a safe base from which to continue learning. And to Evan and Finley, grandnephews extraordinaire, thank you for your joyful perspectives on life, love, and learning. You keep the passion alive.

Marion Porath

To Sophia
i missed her
by a blink, a breath
the beat of a butterfly wing

her secret bare of flesh and bone
blew by my window
her wise old soul looking for home

Karen Meyer

To the students like Lara, past, present, and future.

Anthony Clarke

INVOCATION

In *Speaking of Learning* we devote our conversation to "learning" as if it were both the oldest and newest love in our lives—a mature yet wide-eyed love. The six of us are teachers after all; we regard ourselves as veterans in education. Even so, none of us can say in truth we know fully how learning transpires. For what furrowed paths can exist ahead of time? Rather than rummage for answers inside the modern delirium of education that aspires to reduction, we remain (un)bound in pursuit of an infinite and ethical inquiry into learning. In the following chapters we search and research our life stories, linger in the ruptures and conditions of learning.

Our memories and stories tell us that *school* holds a place in our minds, where we learned school culture, conformity and codes according to time, rules and rulers. As school children we belonged to our first formidable learning community where our anxieties about fitting in outran our brief stretch of experience. Nevertheless we survived school. We foraged awkwardly after truth outside school. And we still do. As teachers and researchers, as well as poets, writers, therapists, and artists, our inquiries tell us that learning essentially concerns finding new ways to be and live in the world, beyond what we know. In this book, the six of us embrace a tangible question inside and outside our selves: what else could learning be?

TABLE OF CONTENTS

Foreword by Hongyu Wang	xi
How this book came to be	xv
Confluences	xvii
I hear the footsteps	xix
The mosaic of teaching and learning	xxi
Conducting an inquiry into learning	xxiii
What led us to writing the book	xxv
Acknowledgements	xxvii
Inner world learnings	1
Life lessons	29
Learning poetically	43
The composition of learning	71
Playing fields	83
What if I had said "no"?	101
Having spoken of learning	115
About the authors of *Speaking of Learning*	117

HONGYU WANG

FOREWORD

Understanding others is wise; understanding oneself is enlightened. Overcoming others is forceful; overcoming oneself is powerful. (Tao Te Ching, Chapter 33)

I have no doubt that many of you who have the opportunity to read this book will be captivated by it, just as I have been captivated. This book is woven through evocative stories told by masterful educators who came together to explore the meanings of learning, teaching, and life. For those who have read *Speaking of Teaching,* the first book publication of their collaborative work, it is not a surprise to hear, again, the profoundly touching, humane, and imaginative voices of these authors. The two books form a tessellation both within each book and between the two, to borrow Marion Porath's (in this volume) metaphor of tessellations to imagine/image learning. My experience of teaching *Speaking of Teaching* (with amazingly positive, even enlightened responses from students) and reading *Speaking of Learning* also forms a tessellation that resonates with a patterned movement of my own temporal and intercultural learning through encounters.

In the opening chapter, Avraham Cohen points out, "Each of us is a current endpoint of our personal and collective history, which drives our teaching and our learning." To go deeper into this history to uncover and understand their own learning and its implications for their educational work is a shared theme of this book. As educators who teach students to learn about teaching, they take on the courageous task of working through their own most intimate interior world to reach new grounds. Such learning is coupled with unlearning. Heesoon Bai shares her wisdom in this volume, "One cannot be a great educator without being a great learner." It is an important call for all educators to hear, not only in terms of aspiring to learn from students while teaching but also in terms of achieving self-understanding in order to become better pedagogical companions to students. What you will read in this book is these educators' embodied journeys of achieving enlightenment about learning, stories that will move your heart, mind, and spirit, and inspire you to embark your own journey, if you have not yet started.

Learning from the past, we can see that many of us had a serious childhood particularly in school, seriousness that has lingered in photos and been stored in memories, clearly or vaguely. As Doll (2012) points out, "Seriousness quickly overpowers our sense of alternative possibilities; it locks us in to the already tried; it limits our perspective" (p. 148). By contrast, play, rather than serious competition that exists in today's educational world, can release new possibilities, take us on alternative routes, and bring vital life energy to learning. It is unfortunate that learning and play mostly do not go together in institutional forms,

FOREWORD

but playing with ideas, things, and relationships is central to education (Aoki, 2005; Macdonald, 1995). It starts with childhood, as the stories of Shaya and his grandmother in Karen Meyer's (in this volume) novel memoir demonstrate so playfully. Wawa, a name given to grandma by a three-year-old boy, means "play." In play, there is a sense of flow that gives way to the process of complex emergence that embraces rather than rejects ambiguity and uncertainty. What if our schools can become playing fields in which students play, like Shaya, with the watchful, patient and compassionate companionship of teachers?

Carl Leggo (in this volume) speaks about "the etymological tradition where teaching and learning are equated" in Old English, German, and Dutch. Confucius is also well known for, I would add, stating that teaching and learning mutually enhance each other. And I trust that he would applaud these educators' efforts to learn to become sages, to become fully human in an ongoing process of learning, teaching, and educating. At the same time, learning and teaching is not in a relationship of linear causality (Bai, in this volume), as a lot happens in a situation of learning both in and outside of the classroom. Particularly in this age of accountability and standardization in education, to tie teaching and learning in a direct causal-effect way kills the spirit of education in its fundamental task of vitalizing students' inner life and external explorations.

Teaching and learning is also a mutual process across generations—child, parents, and grandparents—as Shaya and Wawa's stories show. If "for the most part, parents lead children. Grandparents follow children" (Meyer, in this volume), then the task of an educator—Anthony Clarke (in this volume) prefers to be an educator rather than a teacher—is to both lead and follow children. Education, in its original sense means "to lead out (*ex-ducere*)" (Aoki, 2005, p. 350). Leading students out to possibilities-yet-to-be, educators must also follow students' pathways in their own timing. What Anthony Clarke learned from Lara is that educators must be attentive to learning from students in following where their potentiality leads. In leading students out, educators both learn and teach.

If wounding has been an almost inevitable by-product of schooling, although the specific patterns and experiences of each individual can be different, as Avraham Cohen argues, then listening to what is unspoken is important if we would like students to heal and become whole again. Learning to listen is not only about listening to words but also listening to the unspoken emotions and feelings. Yet such a capacity for deep listening cannot happen in a teaching situation if a teacher, or a teacher educator, has learned to not get in tune with her or his own emotional world. Without such inner work as authors of this book have accomplished, the depth of pedagogical relationships cannot emerge. If there is an ethic of learning in not doing harm (Bai, in this volume), then there is an ethic of teaching in not doing harm. Great educators are also healers. I advocate a nonviolent relationality in education, beyond the dualism of body and mind that heals the wound and advances organic learning (Wang, 2014). Carl Leggo's question, "When I speak of learning, why does fear taunt and haunt me so?" should ring in our ears every time when we enter each teaching setting—whether at school or university.

FOREWORD

How this book came to be is as fascinating as the book itself. The authors formed a group eight years ago to discuss what it means to be an educator and what it means to be a learner. As a result, a community of educators as learners has evolved, and *Speaking of Teaching: Inclinations, Inspirations, and Innerworkings* was written and published. From the confluence of "seeming randomness" (Bai) toward the self-organizing interconnections of the group to "great companionship" of these seasoned educators in *feeling* the individual and collective message of learning, and teaching, and being (Cohen), from "a genuine conversation" that is emerging and generating (Clarke) to embracing learning as "the oldest and newest love in our lives" (Meyer), this book has been born out of these educators' passion for living a worthwhile life together with students. While what they share is much bigger than this book, I suggest that every teacher educator use the book in their teaching one way or another as a springboard to generating insights and wisdom on how to learn, teach, and educate *against* the official and institutionalized learning that is behaviourist, deterministic, narrow-minded, competitive, and permeated by the mechanism of control.

The flow of this book draws me in, touches my heart, and refreshes my mind. The flow disrupts any rigid sense of structure, yet at the same time depends on a certain sense of structure to hold its tension and form a dynamic movement. The juxtaposition of narratives, poetry, photos and artwork, and insights demonstrates vividly this dynamic that cultivates wisdom, nurtures compassion, and inspire enlightenment. This flow is also an exemplar of the group's innerworking and outerworking in a "micro-version of a stadium wave" as Karen Meyer (in this volume) describes. I hope its flow will have a similar effect on you as you enjoy reading this incredible book. Let their words flow into your world to connect across boundaries and nourish new words to speak of learning, teaching, educating, and becoming…

REFERENCES

Aoki, T. T. (2005). *Curriculum in a new key: The collected works of Ted T. Aoki* (W.F. Pinar & R. L.. Irwin. Eds.). Mahwah, NJ: Lawrence Erlbaum.
Doll, Jr., W. E. (2012). *Pragmatism, post-modernism, and complexity theory* (D. Trueit Ed.). New York, NY: Routledge.
Macdonald, J. B. (1995). *Theory as a prayerful act*. New York, NY: Peter Lang.
Wang, H. (2014). *Nonviolence and education*. New York, NY: Routledge.

Hongyu Wang is a professor in curriculum studies at Oklahoma State University–Tulsa. Currently committed to theory and practice of nonviolence education, she has published books and articles in both English and Chinese.

AVRAHAM COHEN

HOW THIS BOOK CAME TO BE

It All Started When…

The Tao that can be told is not the eternal Tao. (Lao Tzu)

… I was a child. Hmm, maybe it actually all started when my parents met. Or, when my grandparents came over from Europe in the early 1900s. No, wait! I get it. The Big Bang was the starting point for this book. I wonder what happened before the Big Bang?

Our group, as I have detailed in our previous publication (Cohen et al., 2012), is a highly gifted, accomplished, and most importantly, a lovable group of human beings. We each represent, as does each of you reading this, the current endpoint of our particular lineage, as well as the collective human experience. Our group is aware that collectively we are a message in our way of being, individually and as a whole. The glue that has held this group together was well summarized by Tony Clarke, who said something like, "I don't need more publications or more work. The main reason for me to be part of this group in an ongoing way is for the opportunity to be with colleagues whom I appreciate and whose companionship I savour." Certainly, our group has provided great companionship, and this companionship has been the personal and pedagogical ground from which this book has sprung.

This publication grew out of a passion for life (inner and outer), relationship, and education. The individuals in this group are committed to living in rich and creative ways, and to sharing this commitment with students—indeed, with anyone who comes within range. Their influence could be seen as about what they know and what they can do, but I know that it is most profoundly about who they are in their humanness and vulnerability.

AVRAHAM COHEN

Only One Word

Being …

Is how this book came to

Be …

Moment by moment by moment …

—a. cohen

REFERENCE

Cohen, A., Porath, M., Clarke, A., Bai, H., Leggo, C., & Meyer, K. (2012). *Speaking of teaching … Inclinations, inspirations, and innerworkings.* Rotterdam, The Netherlands: Sense.

HEESOON BAI

CONFLUENCES

Seeming randomness behind confluence has always fascinated me. Seeming randomness ... and yet, I am surprised to see how the elements that come together can be so generative: the case in point is our group of educators. I have my own separate history with everyone prior to our coming together as a group, with the exception of Tony. The present book has come out of the confluence of random elements I spoke of here. And this is what the confluence looks like for me:

I met Marion close to twenty-five years ago. My first-born and I were introduced to Marion by my neighbour in UBC Family Housing who was then, I think, one of Marion's students. I was a housewife, "homeschooling," that is, learning with, my first-born, Lumina. We became involved in Marion's research project on gifted children. Marion appeared to me then, as now, and ever so, a gentle, perfectly poised, kind and sweet person who was, and is, a consummate academician. Years later, a series of unanticipated events led me, out of the blue, to become a doctoral student at UBC, and Marion and I renewed our acquaintance. Nearly a decade later, this time through Avraham, who became my husband by way of my UBC connection, Marion and I came together again, now as members of our Educators' Group, otherwise known as ePod.

I met Karen Meyer close to twenty years ago, as a new doctoral student at UBC. I responded to a call about forming a reading group for Francisco Varela's work. Meeting her for the first time, I remember being astonished by her vivacity and soaring imagination. Subsequently, when I became a professor myself at SFU, we became involved with supervising each other's various grad students. And then, Avraham showed up in my life, and formed this Educators' Group: another point of connectivity added to my association with Karen.

I don't remember the exact beginning of my association with Carl Leggo. Most likely, it was through Karen Meyer as Carl and Karen were supervising many graduate students together, and I was probably invited by Karen to be on one of their mutual students' supervision committees. But the very first time I saw (but did not meet) Carl was at a CSSE (Canadian Society for Studies in Education) annual conference almost a couple decades ago. I forget whether I was a doctoral student or a newly appointed assistant professor. I happened to go to his presentation: he was standing and reading his poetry in the most animated way. I was transported by the whole scene.

My history with Tony has mostly been confined to our group meetings for the past six years. He is, it turns out, a maverick scholar and teacher of an enormous capacity. (All the members are, really!) And what a marvellous storyteller he is! I enjoyed his story in our first co-authored book, *Speaking of Teaching,* and the story in this volume, too, is a charming school story that documents his own transformation as a teacher.

And then, of course, there is Avraham Cohen, the intrepid leader of our small band of university educators, under whose gentle but persistent guidance we all seem to be on the personal and professional quest "from age-ing to sage-ing^{TM}" (Schachter-Shalomi & Miller, 1995). I still think one of his most memorable lines is: "We teach who we are, and that is the problem" (Cohen, 2009/2014). How he came into my life is another one of those mysteries of confluence that my rational mind cannot fathom. We are so different from each other in so many ways, and perhaps this is why we are very powerful as teachers to each other. We often get mixed up as to who is teaching whom, and get into trouble when we both want to be the teacher! With Avraham, I never know when a learnable moment will show up. I am learning to be increasingly ready!

This book arose out of all the confluences mentioned above, and more. And I am convinced that one cannot be a great educator without being a great learner.

REFERENCES

Cohen, A. (2009/2014). *Becoming fully human within educational environments: Inner life, relationship, and learning* (2nd ed.) (Previous title: Gateway to the Dao-Field). Vancouver, Canada: Writeroom. (Original work published 2009)

Schachter-Shalomi, Z., & Miller, R. S. (1995). *From age-ing to sage-ing: A profound new vision of growing older*. New York, NY: Grand Central Publishing.

CARL LEGGO

I HEAR THE FOOTSTEPS

I am currently teaching a course titled *Teaching Literature*. The class includes 33 teacher candidates who are learning about teaching in order to become teachers, especially teachers of literature. In the process of their learning, they are becoming teachers. Some of them have already spent years teaching in international locations. Most of them have been teachers and coaches and mentors in diverse community contexts. What does it mean to become a teacher? What does it mean to become a learner?

When I ruminate on the phrase "speaking of teaching," I focus much of my attention on my role as a teacher. I was once a secondary school teacher. I taught students in Grades 8 to 12. For more than two decades, I have been a teacher of teachers. Of course, in all my teaching, I am also a learner. I am always learning, leaning into the world with curiosity and enthusiasm. But when I think about myself as a teacher, I see myself as a kind of actor, clown, comedian, entertainer, evangelist, mentor, motivator, performer, poet, preacher, prophet, proselytizer, rabble-rouser, and salesman. As a teacher, I am on call, on stage, in the spotlight. I am public, perhaps exposed and vulnerable.

When I ruminate on the phrase "speaking of learning," I focus my attention on being alone, sequestered with books, wandering in libraries, scribbling in notebooks, staring into the computer screen, pondering and wondering. Learning emerges in private experiences. Learning is often still, ruminative, slow, full of detours.

Learn is etymologically connected to the Old English *leornian*, "to get knowledge, study, read, and think about." There is also a connection through Old English and Old High German to the sense of "following a track" and "the sole of the foot." (Interestingly, pedagogy has similar etymological roots.) Also, there is a long etymological tradition where teaching and learning are equated. There are etymological connections between Old English, German, and Dutch where learning is derived from words that also mean "to teach." Until the early 19th century it was even acceptable to write "he learned me how to read."

So, when I speak about teaching and learning, I am speaking about a life journey. When my father was dying with a brain tumour and I lingered with him for a few days in palliative care, I watched a nurse make his bed. She was precise and quick. I asked her, "Do they teach you how to make beds in nursing school?" She responded, "It's the first lesson." In that moment, I was impressed with her bed-making skills, but I also wondered (though I didn't ask her) how she was taught to care for the patients in her charge, or how she learned to relate to the person who was sleeping and dying in the bed she made with such precise care. I have many questions about teaching and learning.

CARL LEGGO

I am always yearning for learning. I lean into learning, walk the lines like a tightrope strung between here and there, cast my lines into the air like I might yet catch a thought, an idea, a fact even, that will help me in the journey of daily blessing I know as I walk in the earth. I am learning to hear the heart's rhythms connected to the rhythms of each foot rising and falling, sometimes shuffling, sashaying even, almost salsa-like on occasion, even marching when necessary. Speaking of learning is learning to speak, to seek the faint lines of a path that might or might not be there. Speaking of learning is speaking of living, asking questions, becoming human, following the heart's beat with gladness.

I am glad for the rare privilege of journeying with Avraham, Heesoon, Karen, Marion, and Tony. In my journeying with them, I am learning how to teach and how to learn, and I am learning how teaching and learning resonate with the rhythms of one foot falling after the other, one foot following the other, each footstep spelling out a track like a furrow in a snow-filled field.

MARION PORATH

THE MOSAIC OF TEACHING AND LEARNING

Over eight years ago the authors of this book, united by our commitment to and curiosity about teaching, began to meet together to discuss what it meant to be an educator and the nature of the psychological work that underlies pedagogy. A community evolved; stimulating, evocative, and provocative talk prevailed; and a book, *Speaking of Teaching... Inclinations, Inspirations, and Innerworkings,* was written. We couldn't stop. Our conversations continued; we now spoke of the relationship between teaching and learning. We explored our earliest experiences of learning and how these experiences may have influenced who we became as teachers—first experiences with school that shaped us; educational philosophies in our homes; the learning that defined, and continues to define, who we became; the psychological aspects of our identities as educators and where learning experiences shaped those identities. Exploring learning vis-à-vis teaching, and the many related topics that arise, with Avraham, Carl, Heesoon, Karen, and Tony adds immeasurably to how I think about and value life as a teacher and learner.

Now, the second book. It speaks of learning. For me, speaking and writing about teaching and learning privileged me to think about the intricate relationship between the two acts. I have always known, certainly in a more intuitive than explicit way for a lot of years, that, for me, there is no teaching without learning and no learning without teaching. I cannot teach without learning about and from my students; my students learn from teaching each other and learning about me. We learn by teaching, through teaching, and for teaching. Teaching and learning form a conceptual mosaic—fragments of experiences that fit together in a complex, artistic portrayal of pedagogy. My mosaic juxtaposes narratives about my learning —narratives of who I was, how I learned, and how those stories are part of who I am now as learner and teacher.

Creating a mosaic about teaching and learning is especially satisfying now that I am recently retired from a teaching and learning journey that began with teaching elementary school and progressed to 25 years as a professor. The journey has not ended. It is a journey into the light. Moonlight upon the water. Making a new life by building on the old. Magical. I am that little girl who fell in love with landscapes, walked the paths, picked the flowers, scuffed the leaves on my way to school, played in tide pools, found satisfaction in academic accomplishments, loved art and writing—all of this lying dormant in my elder self and awaiting rediscovery. I will take the many pieces from my teaching and learning journey that rewarded and nourished me—the beauty of learning, the deep relationships with students and colleagues, the meeting of minds, the intellectual and personal discoveries—and build, "fold[ing] the past into the future" (Meister, 2010, p. 11).

MARION PORATH

In *Speaking of Teaching* I wrote of how teaching can be artful. Learning, too, is artistic in its composition, perspectives, colours, and unexpected creative moments of discovery and awareness. Teaching and learning can fit together perfectly, as the tessellated pieces that form a mosaic are supposed to do. There is a regular repetition that characterizes a mosaic and can typify some teaching and learning. But there is more to it; events and interpretations can force shifts in regular patterns. Learning grows in the spaces, the movement, the unexpected, and the serendipitous.

REFERENCE

Meister, S. (2010). *Mr. M. The exploring dreamer.* Vancouver, Canada: Read Leaf.

KAREN MEYER

CONDUCTING AN INQUIRY INTO LEARNING

What Else Could It Be?

The six of us show up at the café despite hectic work lives. A purpose persists somewhere behind scouring our calendars to find a few hours, and scurrying off to this or that café to meet, nearly on time. We know (and love) the drill by now. First we check in. Stories unfold. Connections unearth. We entertain the ongoing agenda as a routine guest who wafts in and out of the rambling conversations, inciting a topic here and there.

Avraham acts as bandleader. We require one, even though we are professionals, practiced elders at what we do. Avi taps his (invisible) baton on the table, clears his throat (chakra). Tap … "Hmmm …" A hearty conversation continues around the comfy chairs. I turn up late, as expected, and new hugs ring around the circle, bodies with outstretched arms stand up one after the other like the micro-version of a stadium wave. Hot tea left on the low, small table offers another round. "Cheers!" Café windows lend us natural light. Avi taps his baton (wand) again by way of raising his voice slightly louder than the rest. "Let's start … could we?"

Who would want to conduct this group? We've left it to Avraham, psychotherapist, unconventional, and skilled at group inner-workings. After all it was his idea eight years ago …

ANTHONY CLARKE

WHAT LED US TO WRITING THE BOOK

The two books, *Speaking of Teaching* and *Speaking of Learning,* arose from a small group of educators in conversation with one another:

> The more genuine a conversation is, the less its conduct lies within the will of either partner. Thus a genuine conversation is never the one that we wanted to conduct. Rather, it is generally more correct to say that we fall into conversation, or even that we become involved in it. The way one word follows another, with the conversation taking its own twists and reaching its own conclusion, may well be conducted in some way, but the partners conversing are far less the leaders of it than the led. No one knows in advance what will come out of a conversation. (Gadamer, 1986, p. 383)

Avraham Cohen invited us to join a conversation he wanted to have about what it means to be an educator. The initial conversation was ongoing over a period of twelve months. It continues to the present day, seven years later. As we shared our stories of classroom teaching, we questioned each other about those stories. As such our conversation (and the subsequent books) represents a collective self-study of teaching and learning (Loughran, 2010).

Further, our conversations exhibited a type of emergence (Johnson, 2001) that signals the dynamic and generative nature of a genuine conversation. We learned together about what we did as individuals in our own classrooms. As we examined and critiqued our individual and collective understandings of teaching and learning, we "became present" in our own stories (Osberg & Biesta, 2004) in ways that would not have been possible otherwise. This is the power of conversation. Following Osberg and Biesta (2004):

> We *come into presence* not as we get closer to truth, but as we make meaning, as we take a position. And the meanings we make change ourselves and our world, facilitating a new round of meaning making. In this sense meaning is not present, but always emerging. ... It is only through exposing oneself to ... one's unquestioned ways of doing things ... that innovation can arise, that something uniquely new can come into the world. ... We are therefore constituted or *called into presence* through our meaning making *with others*, with *the* Other, or the *otherness of the other*: with what is different to us. (p. 222, emphasis in original)

This is what we did, what we developed, and what we share in *Speaking of Learning.*

ACKNOWLEDGEMENTS

Our group is most appreciative of Professor Hongyu Wang from Oklahoma State University for her carefully and wonderfully crafted foreword for our book, Dr. Yosef Wosk and the Yosef Wosk Libraries, Museums and Archives Fund for a gracious contribution toward the cost of the preparation of the manuscript, Lumina Romanycia for her very fine-grained attention to the stylistic and copy editing of this book, Gerda Wever of the Write Room Press for her careful work with the final formatting of the book, Peter de Liefde and Sense Publishers for publishing our work, and last but not least, one of our own, Marion Porath, for focused work putting all the pieces together, attending to the aesthetics, and contributing her artwork for the cover and interior pages of the book.

AVRAHAM COHEN

INNER WORLD LEARNINGS

C*ertainly, our group has provided great companionship, and this companionship has been the personal and pedagogical ground from which this book has sprung.*

AVRAHAM COHEN

THE LEARNER/EDUCATOR
I AM
BECOMING

INTRODUCTION

This chapter is about an important truth I learned from studying my own life. Given the pain and struggle I had as a child and young person, despite the fact that I was growing up in a "regular" household with well-meaning and caring parents, I had to study my life closely to really understand why I was having such difficulties. It is no coincidence that I ended up becoming a psychotherapist. And later, I became an educator. I have been teaching in graduate counselling programs for the past 14 years. I see a central piece of my teaching mission to be communicating to students what I learned from studying my own life, which has been in so many ways confirmed by my clients and students. At this point in my life, thanks to all my graduate training, culminating in my PhD studies, I have a pretty good understanding of the nature of the difficulties I was having. This, I wish to share in this chapter. I have four purposes in this chapter: 1) to trace my own personal and educational experiences throughout my life, 2) to show how this shaped me as a person and how this relates to the development of my pedagogical practice thus far (an ongoing process), 3) to provide some possibilities for readers to trace their own development and all the ways it contributed to who they have become, both personally and professionally, and 4) to attempt to influence the thinking and pedagogical practice of educators.

In the next section, I theorize as well as illustrate the theme of what was missing from my earlier years that set me on a course of lifelong study.

TRACKING WHAT WAS NOT THERE

My upbringing was notable more for what was *missing* and less so for what was done for and to me, although I have come to see and appreciate what was done for me as I have progressed with my inner work and my ripening process. It has become evident to me over many years of life, psychotherapy practice, and being an educator that what is common to all suffering is what has been missing and continues to be missing from lives, individually and collectively. At first glance it seems that those who suffer abuse at the hands of others who are bigger and stronger, and not infrequently by those whom children would wish to trust, is a terrible occurrence, and indeed it is. It turns out that the damage that occurs in children as a result of neglect is equal to the damage experienced by those who are overtly abused (Miller, 2005). In fact, the damage that accrues from what is not done is in many ways much more difficult to detect as it is insidiously insinuated into the personality, thinking and behaviour of these individuals. It is damage that is invisible, but nevertheless it is there and the damage is serious, for it impairs the ability of a person to be whole, to function in the world, to find meaning in life, and to form intimate relationships.

Such damage is precipitated by abuse, neglect, or a combination of these. In fact, the adults who are the perpetrators often have good intentions but ended up practising what can be benignly described as incompetent parenting, for they themselves were also subject to less than optimal parenting. Damaged children who become damaged adults contribute to the dis-abling of their own children, and to a damaged and damaging culture. It is a surprising realization that both abuse and neglect have the same effect in the inner world and its outward manifestations for children and for the adults that they eventually become. The root of both abuse and neglect is that the child suffers a wound as a result of what is missing (Schellenbaum, 1988/1990). This wound is the outcome of a lack of love attention, affection, validation, connection, and a sense of ontological security, Alice Miller (2005, p. 5) in her important book, *The Drama of Being a Child,* asks a telling and poignant question:

> I sometimes ask myself whether it will ever be possible for us to grasp the extent of the loneliness and desertion to which we were exposed as children. Here I do not mean to speak, primarily, of children who were obviously uncared for or totally neglected, and who were always aware of this or who at least grew up with knowledge that it was so. Apart from these extreme cases, there are large numbers of people who enter therapy in the belief (with which they grew up) that their childhood was happy and protected.

Miller has captured here the "problem" that afflicts very many of the functioning sane who cannot understand what is the matter with them because surely their daily sense of dread, anxiety, and fatigue is a signal that indeed something is wrong. This wrongness is rooted in their personal history, and that history is an embedded outcome of and contribution to a culture that values all that is other than human. Production and doing are the privileged values. Feeling and being are marginalized. The body that falters is blamed and disliked.

Inner security is a felt sense of knowing one's place in the world and manifests in a confidence that a child and eventually an adult can respond to life as it is, and is resilient in the face of difficulty. I have seen that no one, either in my personal or professional life, has escaped some aspect of this wounding. The task of education and psychotherapy is to assist with healing and recovery from these woundings and to support movement towards what Maslow (1971) titled *The Farther Reaches of Human Nature*. We are not there yet for that understanding. Mainstream education tends to be the purveyor of the cultural norms that continue to be destructive to being human, whole, and happy.

Mark Epstein (2013), the psychiatrist and Buddhist meditator, talks about the need for security and how this is formed. He highlights the need for security, safety, and certainty. He states, "*Pain is not pathology.* It is the absence of adequate attunement and responsiveness to the child's painful emotional reactions that renders them unendurable and thus a source of traumatic states and psychopathology (p. 38). His statement here, based on attachment research, captures the importance of early and secure connection to parental figures, and most importantly, the effect of the lack of this. Inevitably there are disruption experiences to this secure bonding. If the parent is alert enough, then the child will be supported as they go through these experiences. Fritz Perls (1969) put it in slightly different terms. He talked about the importance of frustrating the child in order that the child would learn to deal with difficulties and discover that he or she could indeed deal with troubles, all in the service of preparing the child to deal with the exigencies of the world. The point, of course, is not to torture the child, rather to provide them with reasonable opportunities to practice what will prepare them for life.

A child who is completely protected from such experience will be unprepared for unexpected and unknown occurrences. Alternatively, a child who was not protected sufficiently from the outset will be debilitated by the chronic internal pressure to be alert to dangers of all kinds, and will become someone who cannot discriminate between real dangers and those that are due to their own well developed and unconsciously insinuated parataxic distortions; the propensity most of us have to see what we are used to rather than what is actually there. For those who grew up in circumstances of threat, danger and/or neglect, any circumstance that "reminds" them of their early experience, even apparently small occurrences that may be buried in patterns and outside their awareness, will cause them to experience a reactivation of the whole process. They will consequently apply the early template to the current situation without any question as to whether their reaction actually fits the reality of the situation. The point to be taken here is that both over and under-protection have the same result, a child and eventually an adult who is chronically distressed, who cannot deal with the world as it is, and whose relationships are influenced, distorted, and disrupted by these early experiences noteworthy for their lack of love, care, security, and necessary accompaniment (Cohen & Bai, 2008).

NOTES ABOUT THE WRITING IN THIS CHAPTER

I know there is an energy in the overall gestalt of my writing that conveys a message and that most readers will come away with an impression that resonates at a deeper level than the intellect. I see this as equivalent to the Japanese word *kokoro*, heart-mind, which I will say more about farther along in the chapter. My "approach" can also be seen as relating at the level of *ki* energy, spiritual power. Yuasa (1993) makes a detailed case for how this is the interconnecting force that explains so-called unexplainable experiences. Space limitations will not allow me to go into those details. My point here is to let you, the reader, know that I am writing from a base that begins its emergence from deep within me and is the outcome of the moment as I write, and that moment is the outcome of history that precedes the moment—from the beginning of Time! I am not suggesting that I am an avatar, rather, as Jung (1961/1989) suggested, I am subject to and recipient of the collective unconscious, the unconscious that contains the collective history of human existence. Each of us is a current endpoint of our personal and collective history, which drives our teaching and our learning.

THE CREATION OF THE HUMAN AND NOT SO HUMAN DIMENSION IN ME

As a psychotherapist I don't really fit into the mainstream of the profession that is still moulded by a medical or pathology-oriented paradigm. I am more comfortable within a paradigm that sees humans moving along the continuum of possibility, forever in a state of realizing, realized, and not yet realized. The modern western views of human beings, which form the mainstream, propose that there is something called normal and/or average, and that what falls outside this construction is considered exceptional; such exceptionality is viewed as either highly proficient or highly deficient. Carter (pp. 14–15) writes:

> Most importantly, the insights and personal developments achieved through a practice are not meant to apply exclusively to the particular art through which they were learned but to life as a whole, by extension. One's whole body-mind is transformed by the specific practice, and one now walks and acts in the world differently. One will never see the world the way it was …. To begin to see differently is to begin to act differently and to be different.

The classical eastern views, based from my understandings of Daoism and Zen, suggest that there is an ideal, but hardly anyone is near this ideal, and the possibility for all human beings is to be on the path towards the ideal. My particular view on Buddhist and Taoist philosophies and practices suggests that it is not considered pathological that a person is not at the ideal. If anything would be possibly seen as "wrong" it would be somehow not being on the path towards this ideal. To be sure, this is my view and there are contrary views in both eastern and western philosophy and psychology. Within this view, all practices are seen as having the aim of perfecting the practitioner, and the perfection of the art and the artist are an integral whole (Davey, 2007). In my practice as an educator, and as a psychotherapist, I am interested in cultivating my own movement towards the ideal and in creating conditions that are optimal for this possibility for students and clients. Perhaps it is important to note here, even if briefly, that perfecting being is not to be confused with something obsessive that involves self-loathing.

FOLLOWING THE BREADCRUMBS

I intend to trace here some of my personal history along with my history in school. My purpose is to show how these early experiences influenced my current pedagogical stance, attitude, philosophy, values, and practice. My interest is to support you, the reader, to reflect on your life experience and how this has influenced your learning. I will explicate this within a loose framework that encompasses three major themes:

1. Alienation and Connection: to do with a sense of being connected to no one and nothing at one extreme and to feel fully connected to self and others at the other end; for most, somewhere in between.
2. Community, Relational Development, and Individualism: a sense of belonging and being an integral part of something bigger than oneself, being involved in a process of relational development with self and others, and a felt sense of being one's self in an authentic way. The latter encompasses a whole spectrum, from feeling completely separate from others to feeling connected with others while still feeling oneself.
3. Inner Work and Self-Cultivation: these are the processes of identification of, and work with, one's inner world in the service of personal development towards being a more whole and fully alive person who is engaged with life as it is.

EARLY DAYS

I avoided preschool. I don't even know if there was such a thing when I was at that age. I didn't go to kindergarten. I told my mom I didn't want to. Actually, I was already fearful about being away from the safety and security of home and my mother. I have no memory of being with groups of children, and really, I was afraid of groups of children. My insight at this point of my life is that I had picked up my mother's anxiety about strangers, that this was seamlessly taken in and had the result described. I do have some memories of a group of kids that I avoided in my neighbourhood when I was very small, when we lived on Snyder Avenue in Toronto. I had one small friend, Vanda, who lived across the street. She became very significant for me, at the time, and in memory. When I had the opportunity to meet with her years later, interestingly, she was not at all as I remembered her and she had almost no recollection of me and our relationship at about the ages of three to four.

Just after my brother was born, when I was four and a half, we moved from Toronto, Ontario, to Vancouver, British Columbia, which was a move from the middle of the country to the far west coast. All our extended family lived in Toronto. This move turned out to be a major rupture to my attachment bonding systems that were perhaps already not the strongest. I recall that we lived in the Sylvia Hotel on English Bay in Vancouver for three months while we looked for a house. We finally moved to 27th and Carnarvon where I shared a bedroom with my only sibling, my brother, Stephen. When I was an adult I learned from my mother that there had been a third conception that resulted in a miscarriage; perhaps the sister that I had strangely always longed for, and no doubt this loss had a substantial effect on my mother, which undoubtedly would have affected me and the whole family. This was more or less the culture of our family. I was told nothing, knew nothing, and suspected nothing. Sharing of experiences or feelings, "bad" or "good," was not done in my family. I was protected from this, no doubt, with good intention. I learned eventually that this protection had negative consequences. I was not prepared for the reality of the world. In my own tiny little way I wound up living the Buddha metaphor. The Buddha grew up in a castle. His father was the King. His father was told when the Buddha was an infant that he would grow up to be a great ruler or a great spiritual leader. The King preferred his son to be a great ruler. To this end, the young boy was afforded every luxury and was completely shielded from most of life's realities. As an adolescent he prevailed on his attendant one day to take him outside the castle walls. There he saw things that he had no idea about. He saw a dead body. He saw an old person. He saw someone who was sick. Eventually he saw these three experiences as the suffering that humans might make effort to overcome—sickness, aging, and death. I too was sheltered to the extent my parents, particularly my mother, was able to do this. This sheltering certainly influenced my eventual approach to classroom cultural development and my ways of learning. My learning was compromised as I did not recognize suffering. I literally often did not see it or acknowledge it. When I caught glimpses of suffering, I turned away as quickly as possible. The story of the Buddha is a metaphor for my own story. My approach in classrooms is the outcome of my own inner work that helped me recognize suffering and its impact: my own, through my lifespan, and that of others. My capacity for empathy for myself and for others had to be developed, which it was through the process of my inner work.

Recognizing my unpreparedness for life was important. Coming to an understanding of how this also kept our family isolated was central. We could not form the deep bonds for which the sharing of deep feelings would have opened the way. Such deeper knowing of each other would have opened the door to vulnerability. This was not a value that was held by my family. I came to see that I could provide this opportunity in class by attending to the human dimension, connecting this to curriculum, and overall creating opportunity that was new and eye-opening for students. I still recall feedback I heard from students that "this is the most intimate and close experience I can imagine." What was most surprising was that this feedback came from a base of one half hour devoted to personal sharing at the beginning of every class. There were thirteen classes. Six and a half hours of meaningful connection earned this feedback! I was left to wonder about the state of the world and human connection in everyday life.

We lived in our first house until I was about 12. A move down the hill occurred. This represented a loss of my neighbourhood, and the kids with whom I had essentially grown up. This also meant that I was out of the district to attend the high school that all my neighbourhood friends would be attending. I attended Kitsilano High School, where I knew no one. I don't know that I ever really adjusted to this change; another rupture experience. I went to school every day, about 15 blocks by bicycle. Eventually, I discovered one person, Sheldon Cole, who became my friend, and who lived a few blocks from us. We would ride our bicycles to and from school most days, together. About four years later a high school opened one block from our house, just as my brother was ready to enter high school. I did not want to change schools but I was very envious that he could walk a block to school and I had to pedal all that way every day.

High school was mostly a lonely and alien experience for me. I remember alternating between being bored and frightened while I was there. I was very much an outsider and wondered what others knew that I did not. Everyone seemed to know each other and be friends. Of course, as I found out at one of the only two reunions I ever attended, what I thought and what their experience was, was not the same. Many of them felt as isolated and lonely as I did. I still remember one fellow, Ernie Denney (personal communication, c. 1985, Vancouver, BC), who I thought was very popular and in the center of everything, telling me at the reunion, "I was afraid to be alone. I couldn't stand it." So I began to discover that how things look and how I interpret them is not necessarily the reality of how they are.

What I learned was that alienation, isolation, and loneliness were the common experience. Of course, I didn't know that then. I eventually learned that most everyone longed for something quite different. I found ways to provide opportunity for an alternative and warming experience in my classrooms.

At the age of 14 I began to have some disturbing physical symptoms. I was at first secretive about this, but eventually my fear motivated me to tell my dad. I was quickly diagnosed with gastrointestinal issues, put on medications that made me feel quite sick, and told that I should rest a lot. I was not compliant. I continued to ski and told no one about my troubles. I was subjected to many invasive and for me frightening examinations, and experienced extreme emotional ups and downs over many years. I was very sad and alone. In my twenties, I began to be increasingly determined that this was not going to beat me, or at least I was going to do everything I could to overcome this problem. I embarked on a research project that has been lifelong. I think it is fair to say that I have dealt with this issue to such an extent that it does not have remotely the effect on my life that it does for many who have received similar diagnoses. It was also a huge catalyst for my lifelong research into my own identity, life, purpose, and personal enlightenment. This experience, combined with my family experience of non-disclosure, served to further isolate me and to grow the feeling of fear and the experience of being an outsider, an outsider to others and most significantly, to myself. What appeared originally as an illness eventually served as a signal to search in my inner world for meaning and deeper connection.

WHAT I NOW UNDERSTAND

I will say a few words about my family and the relationships here as I feel this is germane to what I have eventually done in my life both personally and professionally. My parents did everything they could to ensure that I would have opportunity of the sort that in their view would be important for me. I do not believe that they withheld any possibilities. I do, however, think they were limited in their view based on their own background. Their parents, my grandparents, came from Europe in the early part of the 20th century. They were working class, worked hard, and produced sufficient income to feed and shelter their children. Both my parents completed Grade 12 and went to work. My father eventually also joined the Royal Canadian Air Force during WWII. As he put it, "I wanted to fight the Nazis." He was committed to this as he joined at age 26. By that age, he could have chosen not to join. He referred to his time in the military as "some of the best years of my life." He flew East Coast shore patrol as a navigator, and clearly enjoyed the camaraderie and the adventure. He told me once that he would have loved to become a doctor. He never had that opportunity. He and my mother did everything they could to provide me the opportunities they themselves did not have.

I was essentially raised by a single mom during the war. When my dad came home I was frightened by the stranger that he was to me. Over time I got used to him. I was upset by the moves we made along with the previously mentioned ruptures in my experience. The birth of my brother when I was 4 was another shock to my system. I was no longer the fair haired boy. In fact, my somewhat light coloured hair actually turned darker! In retrospect, I see that my parents' argumentative and not particularly warm or affectionate style of relating to each other or to me had a disabling impact.

Eventually, my response to the atmosphere in our home, which I found to be non-stimulating, was also troubling. I began to invite the kinds of responses that my parents were primed to give. I felt alien in my family home, and quite unhappy. Another piece of my experience was my "forced" attendance at Hebrew School, twice a week after regular school and on Sundays. I was ostensibly sent there to absorb something of my cultural heritage and to prepare me for my passage into adult manhood, my bar mitzvah. I hated it, learned next to nothing, and was embarrassed in front of my neighbourhood friends about my attendance at this parochial school. They were all sympathetic, and I think mystified, as to what "that place" was that I had to go to on a regular basis. As my bar mitzvah approached I stated, "I am not going to continue at Hebrew School once I am done, and I am not going to attend synagogue anymore." My next venture into synagogue was about 13 years later for the bar mitzvah of my Jewish girlfriend's brother.

Here I have described experiences with themes of marginalization, loss of religious spiritual possibility, loss of my root cultural connections, an identity of victimization that became increasingly self-fulfilling, and a deep and desperate struggle for a place in the world. As Tom Petty (1991) named it, I was "a rebel without a clue."

What I have tried to paint here is a picture of a boy growing up to be an outsider and whose experiences supported an increasingly reflective perspective about life. Eventually, I learned through my process of inner work/self-cultivation that continuing to blame circumstances and my parents was not going to get me to where I wanted to be. I did not really know where I wanted to be, but over time I became fascinated and absorbed in the process of learning about myself, others, the relational field, and about life. Further, I became increasingly aware that while the details of my experience were unique to me, the processes of severance and separation were a most common experience amongst youth and eventually the adults that they would become. All this influenced my views as to what was missing for myself, the students and the educators with whom I work, and heavily influenced and led to my pedagogical practice based in inner work, relationship, and community development.

AVRAHAM COHEN

THE EFFECT OF MY EARLY EXPERIENCE LACUNAE

What was missing? I was not exposed to a close warm relationship, either between my parents, or between me and either of them. What is the effect of these "non-events," which in some ways, while troubling, may not seem too bad compared to what many live as children? My thesis, based on my experience and what I have seen in others, is that I grew up not really knowing the experience of being "warmly held." This absence coloured who I became in a number of ways. Perhaps, what is important to note here is what I also did not have, namely, a horrendous and overtly abusive childhood; far from it. I was afforded many things, vacations, toys that I wanted, I was taken to events that interested me, I was fed on time each day, I was kept warm and sheltered, I was allowed to play with other children, my friends were welcome in my home, and so on. There were many pluses. If this were an accounting ledger, the "assets" seem to far outweigh the "liabilities." So, why did I suffer so grievously and thrash about through my young adult years and even beyond that point? I think my description of my life and my family is not so unusual and represents many "regular" families. I believe the key missing element that overshadowed all else was the lack of felt connection and the lack of witnessing or experiencing warm caring connection in my home. I believe I may have seen this elsewhere but I was so deeply "impressed" by what I did not see that this blinded me to actually seeing this even if it was right in front of me. I was surrounded by peers who had all experienced to greater and lesser degrees these lacks. I am convinced that this lacuna is so prevalent that it goes without notice, and its significance is lost. The resultant misery that is felt and perpetuated is put down to "just being human." My point is that real humans are awake and caring towards themselves, others, and the other-than-human.

Jean Liedloff (1975/1977) wrote *The Continuum Concept: In Search of Happiness Lost* based on her experiences in the Amazon Jungle with the Yequana tribe. She found them to be the happiest, most serene people she could imagine. She became very fascinated with their child-rearing practices, which she found to be unlike anything she had ever seen or known about. She became convinced that what she witnessed was an enormous missing element in the continuum of human development in most modern cultures.

Here is a small example of the effects of their approach: "Millicent was surprised at the difference between Seth's body tone and that of other babies. His was soft, she said. The others all felt like pokers" (p. x). The mother quoted here, Millicent, was an American mother who had read a draft of Liedloff's book prior to its publication. She had followed what she read in caring for her baby. Admittedly, this is a case of one and the baby was only 3 months old at the time. I have had two students who told me they raised their children according to what they learned from reading *The Continuum Concept*. One child was five and the other seven. They both gave similar descriptions of their children; to paraphrase, "he is quite a relaxed child. He is his own person."

Central to Liedloff's (1975/1977) observations is the "in arms" experience. What she discovered was that the Yequana babies were always next to the body of an adult caregiver. She characterized the "leap" from the womb into life outside the uterine environment in this way: "What a baby encounters is what he[1] feels life to be" (p. 36). For this tribe, what the baby "feels life to be" is a continuous experience of warm body contact, fine-grained attention to its beingness, and a deep sense of security. Yequana babies are only put down when they let it be known that this is what they want. Importantly, as soon as they signal that they wish to be picked up again, this takes place. Everyone in the tribe is attuned to this. So, an adult or even an older child who is nearby will pick up the child if the primary caregiver happens to be not available. This is, of course, a major contrast to what most of us knew growing up. The common view in the West, in fact, is that such behaviour will spoil the child and create endless dependency. The logic of this is really flawed. How insane is it to expect an infant, who is in reality helpless and unable to do anything for itself, to learn independence when all its experience is clearly that it is dependent? I know for a fact that my own mother was exposed to Dr. Spock's (1946) writings about how important it was to adhere to strict scheduling for children related to feeding and sleep. She told me she did not believe it, but at other times she gave indication that she had followed these ideas. My mother had very positive intentions. That is why she would have studied Spock, and I am reasonably sure the reality was she did some of both. As an infant this would have a deleterious effect on the most visceral level. I would not know what to expect. I have no doubt whatsoever that my mother did her best and had my best interests at heart. She and I suffered from misguided, and, as we eventually found from Spock's recanting of his earlier advice along with apologies, well intended information. Clearly, I was not raised along the lines of the continuum concept. In the next section I will describe aspects of my school experience, its effects on me, and how my pedagogical practice was influenced by my experience.

GRADE SCHOOL

At the age of nearly six I began Grade 1 at Lord Kitchener Elementary School in Vancouver, British Columbia, Canada, which was about three blocks from our house. By this time I don't recall being frightened about actually being in school. In fact, I was quite fascinated with some of what went on there. Learning to read was a magical experience. I don't recall learning but somehow I did. I quickly became an ardent devourer of books.

Reading was mostly a solitary activity. I have no recollection of being encouraged or discouraged. I lived in a kind of vacuum wherein I discovered my interests and did not really talk to anyone about what I discovered, thought, or understood. I lived within my own world. No doubt this contributed to my lifelong ambivalence towards being social and being monkish. I still seem to vacillate between these two polarities.

---

[1] At the time of Liedloff's writing gender sensitivity and gender neutrality was not the focus that it was at the time of this writing.

AVRAHAM COHEN

As time went by in grade school, I learned that practically all teachers were female and that it was a good idea that I befriend some of the bigger boys. I was very small and often fearful about being beaten up by big boys. Eventually, I became part of the neighbourhood gang where we lived.

In retrospect I see that I lived in a Saran Wrap and Teflon coated world. My parents, and particularly my mother, did everything they could to protect me from harm and discomfort. This good intention had the unfortunate consequence of leaving me unprepared for the exigencies of the world. When the world showed up with the unwanted, unexpected, and at times the horrible, I was prone to freezing and fleeing; not the most effective responses. I was programmed for protection and not responsiveness in the moment to what life presented to me. My pedagogical approach in classrooms is to create a safe enough container that allows for safe "danger." In this context danger can show up at times as formidable personal encounters, along with the risks that often come with out-of-the-box thinking and creative leaps.

HIGH SCHOOL DAZE

As time went by I discovered that school was easy for me, although I did not really think much about this as I was just doing what I did. I didn't have a sense of how it might be for other kids. By high school I began to feel a little restless and bored in class but I was still very fearful of authority and so I behaved myself for the most part.

School increasingly became a tedious experience for me. I would have preferred to be up skiing, which I did in the inner recesses of my mind as I sat hour after hour in class. I believe this was the beginning of my inner work skills (more to be said about this a little farther along), and perhaps an evolution from my inner world experience when I began to read.

THE WORLD IMPINGES

As a teenager I began to have an inkling of the destructive potential of weapons and human beings. The Vietnam War that I "saw" on television became more real one winter. I was 18 and my friends and I decided to take a bus trip to San Francisco over the Christmas break. Somewhere in Oregon a bunch of kids about our age got on. We began to talk with them. I asked them where they were going. They said, "Boot camp." I asked, "Then what?" One of them responded nonchalantly, "Vietnam, I guess." I was totally shocked. How could this be? They were my age. I couldn't possibly go to Vietnam. I was just a kid! Yet, I knew if I were an American I would be them. I was suddenly very glad I was a Canadian and I was also aware that my life was not really in my hands. I had no idea who was in charge but I was pretty sure it wasn't me.

The point of all I have written so far is that the most compelling aspects of my education had nothing to do with curriculum, aside from learning to read and manoeuver numbers. Everything else of real importance to me took place around school and in other places. Well, this is not entirely the case. The school environment had an increasing effect on me, a less than positive one.

My experience in high school was one of increasing alienation. In fact, I did not know this word then. I increasingly thought there must be something wrong with me. I believed that all the other kids were happy and had lots of friends. I was increasingly troubled and did not have many friends. This lack of being connected to others had a direct impact on what I later developed in my pedagogical practice. By the time I became an educator I had learned that my experience differed from most students' only in the details, not in the process and the general pattern. I came to know that most people with whom I was in contact suffered from a lack of connection and community. To this end I developed structures and processes in my classes that addressed this and provided a rehabilitative experience. All my classes begin with personal process time. My students and I have the opportunity to share our life experiences both in the moment and from our lives outside of school. This has proved to be a vastly well received and appreciated experience, and at times has clearly been healing for some students.

UNDERGRADUATE HELL

I enrolled at the University of British Columbia at the age of 18. To say this was a torturous and incredibly fear-inducing experience is an understatement. I still remember walking into the Chemistry Building at 8:30 a.m., three days a week, for a Chemistry 101 lecture. Very many classes were preceded by a trip into the washroom where I would throw up. After this very unpleasant and worrisome ritual, I would walk into a large lecture theatre where a youngish lecturer with a British accent regaled perhaps some with the mysteries of the periodic table and chemical interactions. I was not fascinated at all, and really had no idea what I was doing there. The only thing worse than the morning lectures were the weekly labs where I was in constant terror that I would spill some dangerous liquid on myself—they all seemed dangerous to me—or light myself on fire with a Bunsen burner. I failed the course. I made no appeal to anyone about the many problems I was experiencing. This just never occurred to me, and since no one I knew had any experience with negotiating a university environment, I had no advice from anyone. It never even occurred to me to ask!

My overall experience as an undergraduate student was quite miserable. I developed an extreme fear of speaking in groups, which did not work well in classes where this was a requirement. I enrolled in, dropped out of, and failed a number of language classes; two years of a language were a requirement for completion of a BA. I finally managed to barely scrape through on this. I was affected to the point that for years afterwards I would go to any lengths to avoid public speaking situations. When I could not avoid even the smallest of requirements I would be in a state of fear for as long as I knew about it until the performance was done. Sometimes the performance was nothing more than saying my name in a group and a little bit about myself. I would experience tightening in my throat, a huge amount of rising heat in my body, an inability to actually make sounds or speaking with a trembling voice, and overall a sense that I was a failure as a person.

Eventually I managed to finish a Bachelor of Arts degree. I started in 1960 and finished in 1968. I had a checkered and spotty career and a transcript that with a few exceptions did not show much academic potential or promise at all. I did finally do a little better in my final year and in a further qualifying year, but I never produced undergraduate grades that would have indicated on their own any great academic potential. My eventual major successes in this realm were a huge surprise to me, although apparently not so to a number of people who knew me well, and who certainly had a much clearer view of my potential than I did.

I came to see that many students were not realizing anywhere near their potential. I have fine-tuned my abilities to notice students' gifts, to encourage their emergence, and to create academic culture and community that encourages all members to notice others and encourage them. I need to add that this is no Pollyanna culture where everything is sweetness. As Robert Thurman (2008) put it, "Reality is bliss!" There is a high value placed on honesty and openness. There is also an emphasis on how to give feedback, tough or otherwise, in a respectful and mindful way.

TIME OUT

In 1969, my application to the Master's of Social Work program was, much to my surprise, accepted. I was set to become a graduate student. Fate intervened, and in my favour. I had applied for a job working with a not yet opened provincial facility for severely emotionally disturbed adolescents. As I found out later, there were 450 applications for only 30 positions. I was offered an opportunity to be part of a very select group. This turned out to be a life-altering decision. The director was an Irish psychiatrist, Dr. Peter Lavelle. Peter, as it turned out, did not believe that psychiatry had much to offer to adolescents. His view was that relationship was important. To that end he hired by two criteria: first that he felt he could work with the person and second that adolescents would be attracted to them. I, apparently, met both criteria. I later found out his assistant was against hiring me as she felt I would be an underminer and that I would not be able to withstand the pressures of the work. Peter did not agree with her. Out of the thirty of us who were hired, there were four whom I later found out Peter saw as questionable. I was one of them. As it turned out I was the only one of the questionable four who survived, and eventually thrived, in the situation. This experience made an indelible impression on me. I have since always been alert to the potential in each person and to what I might do to create conditions within which it has the most opportunity to emerge.

We were provided immense personal and professional growth opportunities as part of our employment. Again, to my huge advantage, there was a tremendous emphasis on our own work on ourselves. I needed to work on myself. Amazingly, I was paid to work with adolescents and to work on my own personal growth and development. The influence this had on me personally is beyond description. I see this experience as core to who I have become and to the development of my pedagogical and psychotherapy practice.

I learned that difficulty was a doorway to my deeper potential. Developing this perspective, which did not come easily, was key, as was the actual growth that came from it. An early and incredibly difficult experience came in my early days at the treatment center as a child care counsellor. After three months of orientation, which was one of the most exciting and liberating experiences I have ever had, our initial intake was eight delinquent boys. I soon found that my early childhood experiences of fearfulness about being beaten up by big boys had been revivified. In fact, at no time was I beaten up by anyone, either as a child or as an adult, but in my inner world the potential was very powerful. The delinquent boys appeared in my inner world like animals on the trail of blood. They smelled my fear and the more fearful I was, the more drawn they were to taunt, torment, and threaten me. All the ideals my colleagues and I held that we would treat them very well, with compassion and understanding, and that this would change them, were mercilessly dashed. I weighed about 140 pounds at the time I started this work. In one month I weighed 130 pounds. My pulse rate was running over 100 most all the time. I was not able to sleep. I was awash with anxiety. I needed a way out. As it turned out, the way out was in—deeply into my inner world.

Zen offers the concept and a way of addressing the living experience of the gateless gate (Cohen, 2009/2014, p. 36):

> The gateless gate for educators is present in their classrooms and at most moments. It is really the barriers within themselves. Its presence is often signaled by an untenable event in the classroom. The way to freedom is through the gateless gate. The process of recognizing and engaging with the seeming difficulty and even impossibility of the gateless gate is a life-enhancing and life-engaging opportunity for educators and their students.

I was right up against a very personal gateless gate. I knew that I was hanging on by a thread, a very thin thread. I gathered up every scrap of energy I had left and did my best to formulate how I would address Peter. I knew he would listen to exactly what I said. If I said, "I can't do this. I have to leave," I knew he would agree with me. I had to come up with the right words, words that were true, words that I could live with. I arranged to meet with Peter, who already knew I was struggling. I came to work early that day, prior to an evening shift. My terror was even higher for evening shifts as there was little structure. It was just me, my fellow workers, and these boys. I walked into Peter's office. I sat down. He looked at me in his usual very direct way. He said with his Irish accent, "Yes, what's on your mind?" I said, "I am not able to function within the environment with the boys. My fear is immense. I have lost ten pounds in the last month. I need help." Without hesitation he responded, "Okay, we will have you out of the unit and you will do administrative work. As well, we have David Berg who has been studying with Fritz Perls[2] coming to work with our staff and to teach Gestalt therapy. You will attend every day."

I couldn't believe my luck. I was being supported to withdraw from a terrifying situation, recover, and on top of that I was being "sent" for therapy. I attended every day, five days a week for six weeks. I learned, as in fact Peter had told me for some time, that what I was really afraid of was not the aggression of the boys, but my own aggression. I learned this in a very visceral way. I came to realize that my fear was that I would kill someone driven by the power of the repressed, unrecognized rage within me. At the very same penultimate moment of realizing my potential to kill, I realized that I did not have to. I suddenly had consciousness, and with this consciousness, I had choice. I had the capacity to do harm or not to do harm. I knew that I and others were safe.

Two months after stepping out of the treatment milieu Peter told me I would have to go back to work with adolescents. I was ready. I had a few dark moments but I somehow carried myself differently. I was no longer subjected to the attacking behaviour. I did not smell of fear. I carried the hot flame of my anger in my chest for two years. I carried it safely. No one was harmed by it. My life energy was liberated. My gateless gate had provided the doorway to more of my deeper nature.

To this end I have encouraged students to face their demons, which in many cases are feelings that they do not like to have. I like to tell the story of the three dragons (Cohen, 2008, p. 90):

> A certain master was sitting in his hut having tea. Suddenly he heard a terrible screeching. There was a banging on his door. He went to the door. He smelt a foul sulphuric odor. Opening the door, he encountered three fire-breathing dragons. He looked at them with eyes wide open. They looked at him. He said, "Would you like to come in for tea?" The dragons said, "Yes." They entered, still breathing foul breath and flames. He invited them to sit down. He proceeded to pour tea. Finally, one of the dragons said, "Aren't you afraid of us?" The master replied, "Yes! But if I run away, you will surely chase me, and if I manage to escape, you will surely return again and I will certainly have to run again. I prefer to meet you directly, get to know you, and find out what we might have to offer each other." (Source lost from my consciousness)

GRADUATE SCHOOL

I returned to school to do a Master's in Counselling at Gonzaga University in 1997 in their Canadian Program. I got in by the skin of my teeth. They said they were

---

[2] At the time Fritz Perls, the founder/developer of Gestalt Therapy, had established the Gestalt Institute at Lake Cowichan, British Columbia, Canada. David Berg, who was a philosophy professor at Simon Fraser University at the time, had gone to the Institute to study with Fritz. Fritz was already legendary. It followed that anyone who had been to the Institute with Fritz was viewed with some awe.

impressed by my experience and that while my undergraduate GPA was below the requirement, they felt I should have a chance. I am forever grateful for that chance. I had great doubt and concern about my ability to perform at the required level, although I very much wanted to do this degree. In retrospect, I believe that I was at least partly working to "rehabilitate" my self-image as a smart boy. I was part of a cohort of working professionals. We met at St. Patrick's private Catholic school on 11th Avenue in Vancouver every second weekend on Friday evenings and Saturday mornings for about two years. My initial fear was replaced by an emerging confidence. Not only could I do this, it turned out I was a top student. I was truly amazed. Increasingly, I loved the experience and looked forward to our weekend classes with great anticipation.

The effect on my pedagogical practice was to increasingly develop my skills at seeing potential in students and to further develop my abilities to form relationships with these students and create conditions within which they would not just survive, but thrive.

POST GRADUATION

When I finished my master's I knew that I wanted to teach in a counselling program along with continuing my private counselling practice. I felt strongly that I had much to share that was of value. I had received very positive feedback any time I did anything within an educational environment. I wanted to test out my ideas and practices. I hunted and haunted community colleges where the required education for teaching was a master's degree. Nothing happened for two years, unless you count my dismay at finding that most of the faculty that I spoke with at the colleges were thinking about and planning for retirement shortly. I do recall coming home on one occasion and bursting into tears. I wondered, again, "What is wrong with me? They are all retiring and I am trying to get my foot in the door." Eventually, the call came from Vancouver Community College. Was I interested in teaching the Introduction to Theories of Counselling for their certificate program? I was both elated and terrified. I did well. Eventually, I was invited to teach group counselling at City University of Seattle in Vancouver, BC, Canada. I have now been there for thirteen years, have been designated at the level of Professor, and am the coordinator for the full-time Master's Program in Counselling, but I am getting ahead of myself. I had a new goal after my success with my master's degree.

HUNTING A PhD

Having now had a taste of a graduate academic environment and having seen that I was extremely able as a graduate student I now wanted to do doctoral level work. I applied to UBC with my 4.0 GPA and excellent references and got turned down three times because "Nobody here can supervise your work." At the Counselling Psychology Department where I was encouraged to apply by the graduate advisor who sat on the admissions committee, I was turned down for having insufficient research background. This was after I had told them prior to applying that I thought

I did not meet their criteria for research background, and was told that my experience would stand in place of this. On my second application to the Educational Studies Department, they offered to forward my application to the then Center for the Study of Curriculum and Instruction (CSCI), which eventually changed its name to the Center for Cross-Faculty Inquiry (CCFI). I received a phone message from Dr. Carl Leggo, who informed me that he was the Graduate Advisor and he wanted to talk to me. We connected briefly by phone and shortly after this I received a very different looking envelope than what I was used to receiving from UBC. It was fat. I opened it with shaking hands and hard-beating heart. I was accepted! I was absolutely ecstatic. I could not believe my good fortune, but it was true. I had the evidence in my hands. I was about to have the opportunity to actualize a part of myself that had been languishing for many years. At the age of 59 I was about to enter into a process for the highest academic degree offered in the academy. I was excited about what I would learn, what I would offer, and what I would learn about learning.

As Karen Meyer (2002–2006, personal communication on numerous occasions, University of British Columbia, Vancouver, BC, Canada) would tell me, "Everyone has gifts. My job is to help those gifts to come out." I love this idea, and its practice. In my case, I believe that the surging that wanted to emerge was very powerful and increasingly so. My persistence to gain advanced academic degrees is evidence of this, even in the face of a very flawed undergraduate career and, as I have sketched above, in spite of difficulties that arose from my particular early life experiences. I believe the life force in me was increasingly awakened and pursuit of a PhD was a particular form this took. As the Tao Te Ching (Lao-Tzu, 1989, p. 68) puts it:

Chapter 16
Take emptiness to the limit
Maintain tranquility in the center
The ten thousand things—side-by-side they arise;
And by this I see their return.
Things come forth in great numbers;
Each one returns to its root.
This is called tranquility.
"Tranquility"—this means to return to your fate.
To return to your fate is to be constant;
To know the constant is to be wise.
Not to know the constant is to be reckless and wild,
If you're reckless and wild, your actions will lead to misfortune.
To know the constant is to be all embracing;
To be all embracing is to be impartial;
To be impartial is to be kingly;
To be kingly is to be like Heaven;
To be like Heaven is to be one with the Tao;
If you're one with the Tao, to the end of your days you'll suffer no harm.

I do not claim that I was in a state of pure emptiness that I took to the limit. Nor do I claim that I maintained tranquility in my center. However, what I did do was step aside from inner egoic constructions that may have sabotaged my dream of an increasingly authentic expression of myself, of which my pursuit of higher education was a core piece. I was able to witness my inner doubts and all too familiar lack of confidence, while still going ahead. I was in a place within that would not allow any fears and worries to stop me. I began to welcome these worried parts of myself to appear as allies and reminders of my mother's worried and anxious self. As well, I allowed the "ten thousand things" to manifest. This manifestation showed up in my pursuit of education that would allow for creative expression of my visions and dreams about human beings, relationship, the inner world, personal growth, and all as intrinsic to pedagogical practice. These were all driven by my life force, which I believe to be synonymous with the Tao. My pedagogical practice increasingly became the work of continually clearing my vision to enable seeing the life energy of students, and creating conditions that would be very likely to facilitate this energy finding its natural direction.

My experience as a PhD student was immensely positive in terms of my personal and academic growth. As time went by, I found out that my experience was far removed from that of many of my fellow graduate students. I began to wonder what the problem was. I could see that many of them were not very well prepared personally or academically for what was required from a doctoral student. I further began to see that as much as the students were not prepared, many of the faculty were even less prepared to teach and mentor graduate students, or for that matter, in my view, students at any level. They did not have the personal abilities to relate to students, nor did they exhibit any signs that I could discern that indicated any interest in teaching or working with students. As well, at times I could see they did not have sufficient background and often little ability to actually teach the material they had expertise with. It became apparent to me that having expert knowledge in a subject did not at all mean that a person could teach it. I was astute enough and in many instances close enough to the academic "battlefield" to observe the political infighting, backstabbing, and very frequent lack of support that faculty, including very good faculty, were on the wrong end of. I began to see that implementation of departmental policy was often capricious and that academic politics and infighting could be very harsh and cold. I characterized the environments I witnessed as full of people with high IQs, lots of knowledge in their field, often little ability to help with the learning in their field, and in many cases lacking relational social skills, not to mention civility. Ethics seemed to be a hot topic for discussion but not one that was always practiced. I came to see that the best position I could have was the one I had: graduate student. I was a hothouse flower. I had the best gardeners on my committee. All the co-authors of this book are people that I met and worked with while I was a doctoral student at UBC, with the exception of one, Heesoon Bai, who was not part of my academic cadre, and who eventually became my wife. They were indeed people who cared and who walked their talk. They were popular with students and I witnessed the price that was extracted at times from them by their colleagues for their skill and popularity. I was mature enough as a person and sufficiently strategically minded to know how to take advantage of the opportunities and privileges I enjoyed as a doctoral student. I don't say this latter with any sense of pride. It was what I needed; guerrilla strategies to do well within the academic context. I began to see how this ability was sorely lacking in many of my fellow students, and how costly this was to them.

I used to give a brown bag lunch talk for students called *Everything You Want to Know About Graduate School That No One Will Tell You*. It was always well attended. Perhaps, not surprisingly, my most striking finding was how unaware students were about how to evaluate the personal dimension of faculty and fellow students, how unknowledgeable many were about the relational field, and how wounded they were as students and as human beings. Of course, I was also discovering that very many of the faculty were not different in terms of knowledge in these dimensions, and how unprepared they were to exercise what was required either practically or strategically.

Pedagogically, I have come to develop classroom environments that lack this dangerous, life-destroying atmosphere. The cultural values are community development, mindfulness, care, connection, deep democracy, encouragement, authenticity, and honesty.

IMPLICATIONS, SELF-CULTIVATION, PERSONAL TRANSFORMATION, AND PEDAGOGICAL PRACTICE

I feel it to be important that I give you the above sketch with some detail that will fill you in on my experience. I have, of course, left out much more than I put in. I could have written an immense amount about my efforts to understand the opposite sex, and my struggles with personal relationships with my friends and with women to whom I was attracted. Suffice to say all this was further grounds for what has emerged and created me into who I am today both personally and professionally. I don't recall exactly when I had the following thought. I know it was while sitting in a high school class. The thought was: "If I ever have a chance to do something about this death-dealing schooling experience, I will." I had no thought that I would ever have this chance. Life is increasingly surprising to me. I have indeed had the chance, and apparently I can do something.

I will not go into great detail about how I set up my classes up and in motion, and how the atmosphere, culture, classroom community, and process is developed. For more detailed descriptions I point you to some of my other writings (Cohen & Bai, 2007; Cohen, Bai, & Green, 2008; Cohen, 2009; Cohen, Fiorini, & Bai, 2013). Briefly, what I do in class is to install processes and structures that attend directly in a regular way to the human dimension in the classroom and that integrate the personal and the curricular. What I have designed and generated is what would have helped me to thrive, come increasingly into life, and to feel absorbed and engaged as a young human being who was also a student. I have responded to what was missing in my educational experiences by developing processes and structures that have the aim of creating optimal opportunity for students and myself as educator to acknowledge experiences in the inner world, the inter-subjective world, the community dimensions, and the other-than-human world. My view is that the classroom offers an ongoing opportunity to learn about deep democracy (Cohen, 2009/2014) and community development, and the implications of and for each individual's participation and engagement (Mindell, 1997, 2002).

SELF-CULTIVATION/INNER WORK FOR EDUCATORS: ENLIGHTENMENT

Educators as classroom leaders have a great opportunity to explore their own identity, their sense of being as a human in the universe, the experience of relatedness, and their inner world. They have an unparalleled opportunity to learn how to live as a fully alive and engaged human being. The process involves attending ever more closely to the recursive and interactive experience that occurs between the educator, students, and all aspects of the classroom environment. Classrooms are enclosed microcosms of life, ripe for experimentation and personal growth.

The themes that I have described above, identity, connection, and community as both reality and omission from my life experience, suggest by implication that had things been different, my development as a more secure and at peace person would have been more likely. I can now say from the perspective of the present moment, and with an enhanced ability to look backwards into my own past, that the difficulties I suffered ensured that I would embark on a lifelong journey for nothing less than enlightenment, which I understand as the fullest possible manifestation of my true nature. As Carter (2008) describes:

> these artistic ways (Japanese *do*) ... [are] a pathway, a road, which is what *do* means, from the Chinese *tao* or *dao*, and [they] also signify a way of life, as in *aikido, judo, chado*, and so forth. None of these is to be understood and undertaken merely as entertainment or distraction: they are all ways of self-development, leading to a transformation of who a person is. In short, each of these arts, if seriously engaged in, is itself enlightenment in some form. (p. 3)

I believe daily contact and engagement in the dao-field of educational environments offers this opportunity and an educator who approaches each moment at school with this view will contribute to his or her own growth and development and to the growth and development of colleagues and students.

Carter (2008) references a conversation he had with Masuno Shunmyo, a Soto Zen Buddhist priest:

> The startling insight that he provided at the outset was the placing of his hand over his heart, in order to seal with a gesture the location of the "mind." I smiled broadly and remarked that most Western people would be surprised to see the heart identified as the seat of the mind. He and his assistant were surprised by this implicit critique of the obvious, and asked where the mind was thought to be located. "We would point to the head, to the brain," I replied, causing a moment of disbelief. "Why would anyone think that the mind was located in the head?" he asked politely. (p. 8)

It is perhaps helpful to know that the Japanese word *kokoro* means "mind/heart; the showing of human-heartedness without an ulterior motive" (Carter, 2008, p. 149). This definition suggests strongly, in my view, the integration of mind and feeling, thinking and sensing, a total and fully felt way of being. This is what is often described as non-dual consciousness, a consciousness that is whole and awake in the moment. The point for educators is not whether or not they have achieved such a way of being that is fully present in the moment, rather whether they are in a process of self-cultivation that might facilitate becoming increasingly present in their personal and professional lives.

I offer here a small example of inner reflection and inner work in relation to what I have written in this chapter. I will write this in the moment as the experience unfolds in the service of bringing this most alive for you as you read. In other words, what you are about to read, while it may or may not be surprising to you, will be surprising to me as I write it, as I have not done the particular inner work that is about to emerge here.

> *I am sitting. My attention is directed into my inner world. It is late in the day and I have been up since 7:00 a.m. I have spent the day at my private psychotherapy practice. I feel relaxed and curious. My body is tired. It is the tiredness of having expended my energy as a full expression of myself. I am surprised by my own alertness. My attention is turning to what I have written above in this chapter. What stands out in the moment in my memory are themes from my writing: themes of fear, isolation, and loneliness. As these themes arise in my consciousness I am aware of a growing sense of heaviness in my chest. My breathing suddenly requires a little more effort. I feel an emergent sadness and a tinge of fear. I can hear the sounds of the city in the background, and I am aware that my wife is working across the room behind me. I am in another world. I am aware of two time frames—the past and the present. From the present I am looking back. I have a slight cold feeling in the center of my chest. Now I am back on the UBC campus as an undergraduate. I know immediately that this cold feeling in my chest was omnipresent in those early years at UBC. Many images of experience flutter through my consciousness; too many to capture. I will share a few. I am standing in line to register. I have no idea what to do. After what seems like an interminable wait, I am at the front of the line. A woman, who seems friendly, asks me what courses I want to take. I am suddenly in a semi-frozen state. I have no thoughts about this at all. I have no experience that would have told me to think about this. I have no idea what to say to her! The next thing I know I am signed up for English, French, chemistry, physics, and mathematics. I stumble off and think to myself, "I guess this is what everyone takes." I am one of thousands of students. I am afraid. I feel sick. I do not know anyone. I go home. I say nothing to anyone. Not one word to one person. I am mute to the depths of my being.*

> *I do recall some aspects of my very first day. I have no recall how I got from home to campus or back.*

As this writing emerges I feel a little removed from the actual experiences I am describing. I do not feel indifferent, nor am I numb. I feel relaxed, sad, but relaxed. These life events do not have the emotional weight for me they used to. Apparently my inner work with all these painful experiences has helped me to come to a new place in myself. The past is increasingly the past. My present is not coloured by my previous pain.

The surprising outcome of my reflection is that indeed I have put to rest some long-term difficulties in my life, I have more evidence that change and growth are possible through inner work and research "in the field," and that the self I used to be has now given way to the more whole self that I am currently. The inner work process I have described above, which is sketched out through specific narratives of my experience, gives examples of images and experiences that represent the essence of my being. They show the process of my emergence as an increasingly whole human being. I am also convinced that the difficulties I experienced in my life, including my educational experience, are different from others' in the specific details, and are **not** different in the overall patterns of experience than most who have been "schooled." I have yet to encounter a student since I have become a teacher, or a client since I have been a psychotherapist, who has **not** been wounded by their school experience.

WHAT HAS COME OUT OF MY EXPERIENCE?

How has my life experience affected who I have become to this point in my life and particularly, how I conduct and participate in education, and how I learn? I can see that the atmosphere of fear, unhappiness, and determination to get to the bottom of what troubled me predominates in the narratives above. However, in line with Moustakas' (1990) heuristic research methodology, it seems apparent that I have been in the Immersion stage and it is clear to me that I must now withdraw into the Incubation stage. My efforts to write on in a clear way are not unfolding. I must step back, let the mud boil up from the bottom of the pool of my unconscious, and give it time to settle, in the service of seeing what lies below. I can describe this process for you but I cannot as yet give you the contents of the process. I am taking a break as of now. I will be back.

BACK FROM THE PAST, THE FUTURE, AND INTO THE PRESENT

What I have learned from my experience is that there are a number of crucial elements that could be attended to by educators specifically and by the education system as a whole. What is beyond the scope of this chapter are the cultural and social elements that are created, reflected by, and perpetuated by the educational system. These elements are core to what constitutes it, as well as indicate, by powerful implication, what is missing there. Suffice to say a culture that "insists" on ever-increasing performance levels and ever-decreasing levels of real care and concern for human beings is culpable for the exponentially increasing incidence of health issues, and individual and collective dis-ease. As well, it is not hard to see that the alienation from self, other, and nature is a product of an education system that does not attend in any meaningful, ongoing, and persistent way to the human dimension in education (Cohen, 2009/2014).

What is missing is analogous to what is missing in the developmental process for many children in the Western world—meaningful connection that nurtures ontological security. Educators have a great opportunity to provide a relational and healing self-cultivation experience.

The key continuum themes that run through my story are:

1. Connection⬅====➡Separation
2. Community/relational development⬅====➡Individualism
3. Inner work/self-cultivation⬅====➡Outer/other directedness

What I have described in this chapter is how I was towards the right-hand side of this continuum in my childhood, adolescence, and into the early and middle stages of my adulthood. These themes certainly represent what was missing in my education and, from my experience, what is missing for a great many students. It is not that these "right-hand dimensions" do not have value. The problem is that I had no sense of choice to be anywhere but where I was. I lacked flexibility, choice, and a developed capacity to move into the "left-hand dimensions." I was not free.

I was alienated in the school environment. I needed help to feel part of the school community. I was there, as were all students, to learn facts. I was mostly good at this and I enjoyed it in my first years. As time went by I became increasingly unhappy. I did not feel much connection with my peers, or my teachers. I came to believe that school was another word for prison. The grey walls of my high school looked like prison walls to me. I came to the conclusion the purpose of school was to keep kids off the streets.

I did not have the concepts or practices of inner work/self-cultivation available to me when I was young, but the precursors were evident in me as I look back. I spent a lot of time in my inner world ruminating on my unhappiness and developing and exploring fantasies about being somehow rescued from all this. I did not have the tools to work in creative ways with my inner world.

I would better be described as an isolate at school than as an individual. I believed I was invisible; that no one saw me. The evidence was clear. Nobody paid much attention to me.

I cannot prove that I represented all students. However, my conversations with students and my observations based on close contact with students when I was in graduate school convince me that what I experienced is a significant part of what very many experience while attending educational environments. Further, I saw that what was true for students was also true for many of the faculty.

WHAT IS NEEDED/WHAT I NEEDED—WHAT TO DO?

We are long overdue for a major shift in education, which really means a major shift in teacher education. This shift needs to move teacher education into centralizing attention to the human dimension in all aspects of education. Educators need to have a much deeper understanding about what actually goes on inside human beings, in both depth and breadth. This particularly means understanding the unconscious. So-called pre-service teachers need to learn to be what Heidegger (Thomson, 2005) identified as central to good teaching, models of how to learn:

> Why is teaching more difficult than learning? Not because the teacher must have a larger store of information, and have it always at the ready. Teaching is more difficult than learning because what teaching calls for is this: To let learn. The real teacher, in fact, lets nothing else be learned than learning …. The teacher is ahead of his apprentices in this alone, that he has still far more to learn than they—he has to learn to let them learn. The teacher must be capable of being more teachable than his apprentices. (p. 168)

I suggest that a crucial addition to Heidegger's idea is that educators need to learn how to model learning about being human. Freud identified the unconscious as the repository for that which was unacceptable to the conscious mind. Most of us are familiar with the idea of repressed memory. As it turns out, this is not a very common experience for most people. However, what is commonly unconscious are patterns of being and acting in the realms of thoughts, feelings, and behaviour, and the rigid fusion of these into ways of being that go against the truest expression in the moment of persons and groups. These patterns turn out to be deeply embedded in consciousness, and this consciousness plays out in thought, emotion, body sensation, and behavioural patterns. The integration is tight and works like a perfectly programmed piece of software. Unfortunately, the program is applied without any awareness or control by the person who is so programmed.

Of course, saying it is time for a major shift in education neither makes it so, or ensures that this will happen. In fact, the ideas and suggested practices I have presented here are at best marginal, and certainly well outside the common cultural perspective that sees education as preparing young people for participation in the highly competitive and economically driven culture in which we all live. To progress beyond the scope of this chapter, a careful case needs to be made for how the practices presented here have the potential to be not only economically viable but, in fact, economically more profitable than the existing paradigm. I will say briefly it seems obvious that students and faculty who are engaged in what is meaningful for them do not need to be forced to study and learn. What I believe is meaningful here is the attention to the inner and intersubjective worlds of these classroom dwellers. And, to address the bottom line, those who are so inspired will work harder, be more creative, and most likely have to be told, "Take a break!" This has been my experience.

Educators need to be supported to understand and facilitate the very real human experiences that are happening each moment in their classrooms. To this end I offer three main areas for teacher education to address:

AVRAHAM COHEN

1. Education for consciousness development is central. Perhaps this is better thought of as sensitivity and awareness development that will support an educator to be more attuned to themselves in an in-depth way. Along with this personal attunement, educators will also learn to be able to work with what they discover about themselves that impairs this ability within them.[3] Being involved in such a personal attunement process in an ongoing way will support the well-being of the educator and will support their ability to know their students in a substantial and meaningful way.
2. Understanding and facilitating the community development aspect of the classroom[4] will optimize the learning possibilities for students in two major ways. First, they will learn about themselves in relation to a group. Second, the level of safety will be increased as students connect and know each other in a substantial and in-depth way. This increases the emotional safety within the environment, which has the effect of increasing students' ability to actually attend to and learn curriculum content.
3. Developing abilities to integrate course material with personal experience and practical application will enhance student learning, the meaningfulness of student experience, and give them the sheer joy of knowing that what is being learned applies to their life.

CONCLUSION

I have attempted in this chapter to describe some germane aspects of my own schooling experience and relate this to my developmental process that included relational "insults," intended or not. My purpose in relating this extended narrative of my own life is based in my belief that while the content of my experience is unique to me, the process and pattern are not. I have heard many stories from students and my psychotherapy clients that tell me that wounding within educational environments is very common, and that such wounding builds on wounds from their family of origin, institutions, religious background, peers, and culture. What I have written is to address, acknowledge, and help readers recognize more profoundly their own experience and how it has impacted their identity and consequently their lives. I am not under any illusion that what I write will effect a major change in education, but I am hopeful that it will reassure some people that they are not crazy or alone in having the experiences they have had, or in the effects of these experiences. My highest dream is that perhaps a few more educators who work within teacher education will take note and reflect increasingly deeply on what such education needs to include and how this can be implemented. I believe that peaceful vibrant teachers will cultivate peaceful vibrant

---

[3] For a detailed description of such inner work I refer you to the chapter "Dreaming Life: Working with a Personal Dream—On My Own" in my book *Attending to the Human Dimension in Education: Inner Life, Relationship, and Learning.*

[4] I refer you to the chapter "Classroom as Community: Deep Democracy in Action" in my book cited in footnote 3 above.

classrooms and that students who are emerging from such classrooms will go out into the world and make a substantial and meaningful difference within their own families and communities.

> *Peaceful and Vibrant*
> Two words
> Denoting full aliveness
> Surrounding
> A core of stillness
> Emptiness that is not vacant but fully open to life's potential
> Simultaneously expressed and received.
> —a. cohen

REFERENCES

Brazier, D. (2002). *The feeling Buddha*. New York, NY: Palgrave.

Carter, R. E. (2008). *The Japanese arts and self-cultivation*. Albany, NY: State University of New York.

Cohen, A. (2008). Following the breadcrumbs to the end of ultimate meaning. *AntiMatters, 2*(3), 87–94. Retrieved from http://anti-matters.org/0/main.htm

Cohen, A. (2009). *Gateway to the Dao-field: Essays for the awakening educator*. Amherst, NY: Cambria.

Cohen, A. (2014). *Becoming fully human within educational environments: Inner life, relationship, and learning* (2nd ed.) (Previous title: Gateway to the Dao-Field). Vancouver, Canada: Writeroom. (Original work published 2009)

Cohen, A., & Bai, H. (2007). Dao and Zen of teaching: Classroom as enlightenment field. *Educational Insights: On-Line Journal of the Center for Cross-faculty Inquiry in Education, 11*(3). Retrieved from http://einsights.ogpr.educ.ubc.ca/v11n03/articles/bai/bai.html

Cohen, A., Bai, H., & Green L. (2008). An experiment in radical pedagogy: Enactment of deep democracy in a Philosopher's Cafe. *Radical Pedagogy, 9*(2). Retrieved from http://radicalpedagogy.icaap.org/content/issue9_2/cohen_bai_green.html

Cohen, A., Fiorini, K., Culham, T., & Bai, H. (2013). The circle of leadership integrity within business organizations. In W. Amann & A. Stachowicz-Stanusch (Eds.), *Integrity in organizations: Building the foundations for humanistic management*. London, UK: Palgrave MacMillan.

Davey, H. E. (2007). *The Japanese way of the artist: Three complete works on the classic tradition*. Berkeley, CA: Stone Bridge.

Epstein, M. (2013). *The trauma of everyday life*. New York, NY: Penguin.

Jung, C. G., & Jaffe, A. (Ed.). (1989). *Memories, dreams, reflections* (R. Winston & C. Winston, Trans.). Toronto, Canada: Vintage. (Original work published 1961)

Lao-Tzu. (1989). *Tao te ching: A new translation based on the recently discovered Ma-wang-tui texts* (R. G. Henricks, Trans.). Toronto, Canada: Random House.

Leggo, C. (2008). Narrative inquiry: Attending to the art of discourse. *Language and Literacy, 10*(1). Retrieved from http://ejournal.library.ualberta.ca

Liedloff, J. (1977). *The continuum concept: In search of happiness lost*. New York, NY: Perseus. (Original work published 1975)

Magid, B. (2001). *Ordinary mind: Exploring the common ground of Zen and psychoanalysis*. Sommerville, MA: Wisdom. (Original work published 2002)

Maslow, A. H. (1971). *The farther reaches of human nature*. Hammond, UK: Penguin.

Miller, A. (2005). *The drama of being a child: The search for the true self*. San Francisco, CA: John Wiley & Sons.

Mindell, Arnold. (1997). *Sitting in the fire: Large group transformation through diversity and conflict.* Portland, OR: Lao Tse.

Mindell, Arnold. (2002). *The deep democracy of open forums: Practical steps to conflict prevention and resolution for the family, workplace, and world.* Newbury, MA: Hampton Roads.

Moustakas, C. (1990). *Heuristic research: Design, methodology, and applications.* Newbury Park, CA: Sage.

Perls, F. S. (1969). *In and out the garbage pail.* Gouldsboro, ME: Gestalt Journal Press.

Petty, T. (1991). Into the great wide open. On *Into the great wide open.* [CD] MCA Records.

Schellenbaum, P. (1990). *The wound of the unloved: Releasing the life energy.* Dorset, UK: Element Books. (Original work published 1988)

Spock, B. (1946). *The common sense book of baby and child care* (1st ed.). New York, NY: Duell, Sloan, and Pearce.

Thomson, I. (2005). *Heidegger on ontotheology: Technology and the politics of education.* New York, NY: Cambridge University Press.

Thurman, R. (2008, April). *Buddhism as a civilization matrix and the current global crisis.* Public lecture conducted at the University of British Columbia, Vancouver, BC.

Yuasa, Y. (1993). *The body, self-cultivation, and ki-energy.* (S. Nagatomo & M. S. Hull, Trans.). Albany, NY: State University of New York.

HEESOON BAI

LIFE LESSONS

I am convinced that one cannot be a great educator without being a great learner ...

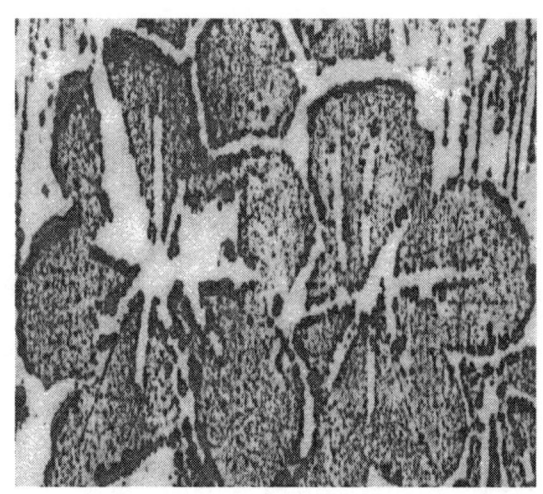

HEESOON BAI

LIFE AS CURRICULUM AND PEDAGOGY

PREAMBLE

We learn all kinds of things, from the moment we pop into this plane of existence (or even before) till we pop out of it. Learning is a pervasive and expansive phenomenon for humans. But not all learning is the same. Some learning is delightful, joyful, beautiful, and animating; some insightful and mind-expanding; some downright "wrong"; some useless; some boring; some hopeless and depressing; some hurtful and harming. For sure, not all learning is helpful. Helpful learning is an ethical practice. Ethics aims at bringing about a flourishing of the world, in which individual beings singly *and* collectively find relief, reconciliation, healing, rejoicing, hope, compassion, and wisdom. It is my hope that we can increasingly bring about such learning in our learning institutions, our homes and workplaces. We need to see this happen, urgently, as we face deepening trouble on all planes of existence: environmental, social, academic, professional, and personal.

In the meantime, I turn to my life, spanning many decades and two continents, to reflect on and see if there has been ethics learning that I can share in these pages. Ethics learning? My readers may ask: "What are you talking about?" I like how the primatologist Frans De Waal (2005) defines ethics as the question of helping or harming. Are we helping or are we harming? Am I helping or am I harming? Seemingly clear and simple questions, but there aren't always equally clear and simple answers. Therein lies the need for us to live and learn, make mistakes and relearn, and pass on what we know. Most often, it takes individuals a lifetime to figure out what's harming and what's helping. Thus, sharing the learning stories of our lives is very helpful to each other. This is what communities are for, isn't that so?

"WHAT DID I LEARN IN SCHOOL TODAY?"

Here is a story of how my formal learning began. This story is reconstructed from my own somewhat vague memories and stories told to me by my mother.

Many children play the game of "school" amongst themselves years before they actually show up at school as a Grade 1 student. Nowadays, young children even go to preschool and kindergarten. Thus when they show up at their elementary school, they already know something about the game of schooling. Not I. I never went to a nursery school, preschool, or a kindergarten. I don't know if they had such things in Korea when I was growing up in the fifties and sixties. And I didn't have anyone in my family to explain to me what going to school was about, or to prepare me for it. Neither my parents nor my grandparents went to school, which was usual for Koreans in those days. My parents grew up without electricity or car or telephone. They were of the generation that was just beginning to participate in the modernization and westernization seeping into the country. This was in the early 20th century in Korea. My parents and my four older siblings went through the period in which Korea was under Japanese colonial rule (1910–1945) and subsequently, the Korean War (1950–1953). As the youngest, I was the only child who did not experience Japanese colonial rule and the Korean War.

I was clueless. Hence, when my mother and whoever else marched me to school on the first day, and tried to have me line up with other children in straight rows in a gigantic schoolyard, while all the parents stood behind the assembled children, I thought something terrible was happening to me. I had never in my young life been separate from my family members in a public space. I wouldn't let go of my mother, and after some struggle, they (I don't remember who) managed to separate me from my mother, and placed me in the assembly. Terrified, I sobbed the whole time, while the principal was giving an edifying and moralizing speech to the assembly of children and parents. That was my first day of school.

In recalling this story, what strikes me most is how the modern institution of schooling shapes the subjectivity of children. Though my own case may be extreme, and most children may fare better than I did in coping with their first-time immersion in school, I would make the argument that the institution of modern schooling represents a critical event of bonding rupture and dislocation in a child's life. (Does it always have to be that way? I don't think so. But we have to know what we are doing.) A child now has to leave the family, the comforting and familiar nest of nurture and care, and enters an impersonal institution that demands that children individualistically compete, fear failure, and work for and earn their keep and others' approval. They now have to justify their existence by demonstrating their extrinsic worth in the eyes of others. They are now open to the critical gaze of society through their meeting or not meeting its expectations as carried out within schools. The survival game has begun in earnest.

It took me about three years before I clued in to the schooling game. Maybe this is how long it took me to become resigned to the existential sign: NO EXIT. The only way out was by staying in and finishing. I must have also finally figured out that going to school was the only survival game in town and that I must learn to play it well, if I was to survive. I survived the first three years, thanks to my mother's singular effort to support me and also to my homeroom teachers' kindness.[5] For my mother, it would have been her survival game, too. A Korean mother's job description includes being a cook, coach, counsellor, nurse, cabdriver, and maybe even a security guard for her children while they go through the gruelling K-12 system.

Why did it take me so long to make sense of school? Probably the best way to understand the situation is that I was in some kind of culture shock. As the youngest of the five (my sibling closest in age was my sister who was nine years

---

[5] It was typical of elementary schools in Korea in the sixties that a homeroom teacher would teach all subjects to her or his pupils. Pupils stayed in the same classroom all day with their homeroom teacher. This arrangement changed when we went to junior and high school. Students stayed in the same homeroom throughout the day but different subject matter teachers visited each class according to the timetable.

older), I grew up like an only child in a family that was in many ways still in a state of pre-modernity. I spent the days playing with my ancient grandmother and pottering around the sprawling household, watching others, mostly adults, going about their business or visiting with each other. I was fed, clothed, and talked to by whoever was around—and there were lots of people, all adults, around, not everyone my own immediate family member: I was free to run about, come and go as I pleased, and to poke around within the confines of our large household. Hence the idea of being made to sit at a desk and perform learning tasks, with a roomful of little strangers, and being told what to do, and most of all, that I had to compete with other children in my learning, was more than my freely wandering little mind could fathom. It was, I am sure, decisively unnatural to me.

Since I was clueless about what I had to do, let alone able to comply with all the instructions, my mother came with me to school every day. She got permission from my kind teacher to sit at the back of the classroom, screened by some large object so as not to distract other students, and attended to the teacher's instructions. In particular, it was my mother's task to remember (she herself was illiterate, although, I swear, she was one of the smartest people I ever met) what the homework was, and upon coming home she tried to have me work on my homework. There, too, she was not too successful as I did not want to do it or perhaps, again, I was clueless. I remember a typical scene at home. I would be eating my apple, enjoying my snack, while watching my mother and my sister busily colouring pictures of apples and cutting them out. They were doing my homework! This whole thing of my mother coming to school with me and doing my homework seems to have lasted for the first six months of schooling.

Eventually, by Grade 4, I clued in, and became a competitive student who stayed up regularly till past 10 pm, studying and preparing for the first major hurdle: the entrance examination for junior high school, which would largely decide one's fate as to which university one would eventually enter. All Korean universities were, and still are, clearly ranked: number one, number two, number three …all the way down to the bottom. For a girl, entering a top-ranked university would determine how well she would fare as a woman, since her choice of husband, his job security and his social standing had everything to do with which top-ranked university she could successfully enter and there meet her future husband. At least, such was the rationale traditional Korean society laid out plainly to its citizens.

"Little girl, what did you learn in school today?" Little Heesoon would answer (if she could): "I learned that for me to succeed in life, I have to compete, becoming a winner over my fellow students. I must get to the right university so that I can find a husband with social standing and wealth. I learned today that all knowledge comes with a price tag. Knowledge from the West has the highest price tag."

Fortunately, along the way, Heesoon also learned many other valuable things, too, even though they were not really part of the official or the prioritized part of the curriculum: making friends, the pleasure of reading, of making art, expanding the mind through reading widely, and the habit of disciplined study.

UNLEARNING TO LEARN AND LEARNING TO UNLEARN

Each time we open our eyes, look at the world, and make sense of the world in certain ways, we have invoked a learning event that took place in the past. The present would be unrecognizable if we cannot see the past in it. Thus, to see the world anew, and make sense of the world differently, past learning has to largely die and recede, and new learning has to be born. But the past does not die easily. It too has its own survival instincts. It insists on persisting. And most often, no insistence is necessary. It has no rivalry, no competition, from the present. As long as no one or nothing disagrees or conflicts with how one has made sense of the world in the past, the past continues to live into the present. Why not? That's efficiency. No need to change when change is not called for. However, now and then, here and there, we may run into someone or some situation that questions and confronts our past learning. These are moments of opportunity for new learning to take place. That is, if we are willing to unlearn what is already there.

Take heed. Every conflict, disagreement, surprise, discomfort, and pain is an invitation for new learning to take place. A new world is born to us. Such moments are unforgettable. Here I share with you one significant story of unlearning from my life.

I had my cultural conditioning: what I imbibed from the culture, small and large, around me, implicitly or explicitly. As an Asian mom at heart, I was rather insistent on our two little girls learning to play a musical instrument—in our case, a piano. My husband and I had little money in those days, but I was committed to giving them piano lessons. We found a qualified piano teacher, and she would come every week to give the girls lessons. My older one, Lumina, was a little more obliging. Perhaps she did not want to engage in conflict with me so as to protect my taut nerves, or hers, or both of ours. Even if dispassionately, she seemed to do her practice every day, at least for a while.

But my younger one, Serenne, who was a feisty 5-year-old then, was not going to be pressured by me about practicing every day. I was not happy about my daily campaign of pressuring my child, but I was not going to—was not ready to—give up the cherished idea of my children learning to play the piano. After all, pressuring one's child to study more or harder was what all normal Korean (and other Asian) mothers were programmed to do by their culture.

One day, after being yet again nagged and badgered by me about practicing the piano, my younger one decided to confront me. She said: "Mom, I think you are more interested in playing the piano than I am. Why don't you take the lessons yourself?" These words, and the bold and decisive manner in which they were spoken by a 5-year-old child, had a direct and penetrating effect on me. That moment of encounter stopped me dead in my tracks, and forced me to look at myself. She was basically declaring that she was not me, and I was not her. I saw, with startling clarity, that my own child whom I loved dearly, who—as the expression goes—was my flesh and blood, was truly a person of her own with independent thoughts, perceptions, and feelings. At that moment, I woke up, at least a little, from my own cultural conditioning. I didn't have to do what I was socially programed to do.

I said to Serenne: "Okay, no more practice pressure from me. But having a piano teacher means having to practice regularly. That's how that system of learning music is set up. So, no practice means no piano lessons. I cannot afford to have a teacher come every week when you don't practice." Serenne was just fine with the idea. What was intriguing and wonderful was that she did not stop playing. She played her piano when she wanted to, which was erratic but frequent enough for years to come.

Many years went by. One year before I finished my doctorate, I secured a teaching position at Simon Fraser University and started to teach. I purchased my first home near the university, and my family of four, including my mother who was rapidly declining in her physical and mental health, moved in. And my girls, who were homeschooled for most of their younger years, were trying out public high school. One day, my now teenage Serenne said to me that she wanted to take up piano lessons again. She said that she was inspired by a Korean girl in her class who was doing Grade 10 Royal Conservatory piano. Okay, I said, and we found a piano teacher for her in our new neighbourhood. The new piano teacher assessed Serenne's level and told her that she could now go into Grade 8 Royal Conservatory piano. The last time she was taking lessons, she was in Grade 4! Interesting. So she managed to "self-teach" for four grades through just hanging out and playing her piano? I was astonished. Serenne excelled and graduated from the Grade 8 level with two silver medals. Was she then going to continue on? I got excited. I was more than willing to support her going on. No, she said. She had had enough for now. "Okay," I said, "As you wish." To this day, she still plays her piano, when she wants. More recently, she added guitar playing, and composing songs and singing, to her music making.

Are there morals to this story? I can think of a few: Never compel anyone to learn. Invite, suggest, and propose, but never demand that they learn; never "make" them learn. Even so, be careful. Any time we have this desire for others to learn something, we need to ask ourselves: whose needs am I trying to address and meet?

WHO TEACHES? WHO LEARNS?

Many teachers like to think that their teaching is directly related to their students' learning. I don't need to deny that sometimes, or perhaps often, this happens. That's a good thing.

However, there are many things in life that are not learned by such linear causality. In fact, there is a sense that profound things in life are not learned that way at all. I relate two stories here: one that I heard from a Zen teacher, and another from my own home life.

Zen Roshi Reb Anderson from San Francisco Zen Center told this story during a weekend retreat I did with him over two decades ago. He spoke of one of his revered teachers in Japan whom he would visit whenever he was there. One year, he went to see his teacher. The usual formal meeting was arranged, and he was received into a room where his teacher was seated. This time, though, something was terribly different. His teacher was in his usual formal robe, and was immaculately dressed. All was the same except that his eyes were vacant and drool trickled out of the corner of his mouth. As he looked at his teacher's expressionless face, Roshi Anderson was struck by a profound question: *What is Zen*? And as soon as this question arose, he was also struck by an insight: "I realized that even in this state he was still teaching me!"

What sense do we make of Roshi Anderson's statement? Surely his demented teacher was not engaged in teaching, was he? But, says Roshi Anderson, he was having a profound learning experience in the presence of his teacher at this particular time and place. Roshi Anderson could say that he learned something important in the presence of his teacher, and *therefore*, his teacher was teaching.

The Zen worldview does not isolate individual objects (including people) from the context and environment within which these objects show up. In fact, it would be fair to say that in the Zen worldview, there are no objects in the sense of separate, discrete, atomistic entities. Existential objects are part of the field phenomena that emerge all together moment by moment. Who I am at this moment and in this place is not separate from this moment and this place, which coexist interdependently with everything else in the universe that shows up at this precise moment and in this particular place. No more, no less.

So, there was Roshi Anderson who was looking at his teacher, and experiencing a moment of profound learning, and there was his demented teacher whose presence was critically linked to Roshi Anderson's profound learning. Teaching and learning are two terms of a relational equation. Whoever sits on the side of learning is a student; whoever sits on the other side is a teacher. The student, ever grateful for teaching that guides his or her life, honours whoever sits on the other side and calls him or her a teacher.

One time I too was in an inexplicable and inexhaustible place of learning. My demented octogenarian mother, whom I was taking care of at home, said something so startling that I did a double take, and at that moment, I had a profound learning experience. Both severe osteoporosis and Alzheimer's disease took hold of my mother in her 80s, which rendered her immobile, incoherent and mostly speechless. On my side, I was completely exhausted from sleep deprivation while carrying on the triple duties of working full-time, raising my girls, and taking care of my mom at home. One day, I was changing my mother's diaper, and out of nowhere, my mother said that she could not die just yet because she needed to take care of me! It was one of those moments when I did not know whether to laugh, or cry, or what. My mother had to depend on me so totally for absolutely everything, except still breathing on her own, and here she was talking about taking care of me. Surely, I thought, she was joking. But then, the possible truth of that statement began to gradually sink into me. My mother dedicated her life to taking care of her children, and raising me, her youngest child, was her last project. Probably even her dementia couldn't stop her indomitable spirit and absolute devotion. Besides, the opportunity for me to take care of her, however challenging and difficult it was, promoted my own growth as a compassionate human being. I was not particularly talented in that department of learning. Caring for my mother gave me the opportunity to practice my compassion and gratitude. In the way Roshi Anderson said that his demented teacher was still teaching him, I would say that my mother was still teaching me, in her profoundly demented state, the lesson I needed most in life: how to be compassionate.

A TASTE OF BLISS IN LEARNING

It is still somewhat a surprise to me that I am a writer. The surprise part is: How did I become a writer and come to like writing when writing experience or practice was lacking during my 12 years of going to school in Korea? In addition, once I came to Canada, I learned to write again in English as my second language, a challenging and laborious process. What was there in my formative years that possibly encouraged me to be a writer, or at least gave me a taste of writing that perhaps stayed with me?

One learning experience comes to my mind, not readily, as it was a rather strange and obscure experience. But the more I think about it, the more it holds the possibility of being a deeply influential event.

Amongst the multitude of fifteen to twenty subjects (the exact number escapes my memory) we were required to take in high school, there was a subject called "Composition." I do not know why this subject was separate from "Korean Language Arts." It was just there, and the teacher taught it, and students studied it. Now, the most interesting part is that in our case, neither the teacher taught nor the students studied in the usual way. The usual way meant studying a textbook under the teacher's instruction, memorizing it, and being tested. None of this took place in our composition class. Instead, what we were told to do was to just write and fill up our notebooks! Every week, we would bring our notebooks to the class, pile them on the teacher's desk, and all he did was flip through each notebook—not really reading it—go to the last page of our writing, and put his stamp on it. For all I know, the teacher wasn't really interested in teaching us composition, or maybe he had other things to do, and decided to use the hour just to keep us quietly occupied. Chances are that he didn't have any curriculum or some brilliant and intriguing pedagogical reason behind the way he conducted the class. Or perhaps he did!

What happened to me is that I wrote and wrote. I filled pages and volumes of notebooks, unhindered by the need for and worries about studying, doing well, and earning a good grade. This was the only subject in which I was totally free to explore whatever I wanted in the way of writing. I wrote little stories, diary entries, letters, and essays. Since I was not being tested and graded, I didn't really care how I wrote. I didn't worry about writing well or writing badly. I just wrote. It engaged my tender, growing teenage girl's soul.

Many decades later, this summer, when I was teaching an undergraduate course, my students and I read an article by an English professor who was advocating writing for no reason other than just for the experience of writing (Yagelski, 2009).

He had some compelling theorizing to go with this practice, using heavy-duty words like "ontological." Writing for Being! As I was reading that article, many light bulbs went on brightly in my consciousness. That's it: my composition class experience was just that. It was a rare taste of intrinsically motivated learning. I was not compelled to study something, was not studying in fear lest my grades drop and I lose my place in the competition. To a captive soul like me, freedom in learning was intoxicating. Bliss. Perhaps it's that taste of bliss that's still lingering around when I write, even when I was writing under the pressure to publish to get tenure.

EMBODIMENT

We are said to be living in a disembodied culture. In the academy, the theme of embodiment is taking off like wildfire. Everyone wants to be embodied. We shudder at the state of disembodiment said to be profound in the academy. I heard a colleague of mine quipping, dramatically, to make her point: "A human being is really a big brain on a pair of legs that move the brain around from point A to B."

Nowadays, we spend a lot more time sitting than moving around, which is linked to increasing cardiovascular disease, if not the likelihood of early death. Even more than the concern about shortening lifespan and precipitating disease, my primary concern with disembodiment is the diminishment of the self and personhood. What do I mean by this? Simply put, to be disembodied is to not know my self because I am not totally present in my being, for my self and to my self, in the most sensate and feeling ways. Descartes' "I think, therefore I am" (cogito ergo sum) is a brilliant statement of disembodiment. An existential statement of embodiment would be: I feel, therefore I am (sentio ergo sum). It is primarily through feeling that I know my being. And feelings are extremely complex and dynamic, and to know them requires that we pay attention to them. Subtle energetic, sensate, emotional, and somatic currents and undercurrents constantly, moment by moment, circulate around in the subjective field of self. To know myself is to be in touch with these currents and understand their sensate signals. Disembodiment means that I am not in touch with these currents and therefore, I am not in a position to know myself.

Embodiment is not about just "having" a body. If that were the case, then there would be no concerns about disembodiment, as we all have bodies. But the language here betrays the truth: "having a body" is a disembodying relationship with oneself, as "having" is an external relationship between a subject and an object. It is not an internal relationship of intimately experiencing oneself from within *this* fleshy fluid being. To be embodied means to *feel intimately from within* the vast sensate ocean of fleshy beingness with all its currents and undercurrents.

There are many obstacles to embodiment. Whenever we are overwhelmed by shock, trauma, and/or emotional wounding, our nervous system is unable to handle the stimuli, and shuts down. This is the instinctual way that our nervous system handles what it cannot handle: by not feeling. I have heard about people going suddenly blind on the spot when having to witness terrible atrocities committed towards their loved ones. Or losing their memory of things that were traumatizing. We experience this in everyday life, too, to a smaller degree, like losing one's voice when too scared or enraged to speak. Or when rushing madly about doing tasks under great time pressure, afterwards we hardly remember many of the details of what we did. Imagine living one's whole life more or less that way: not being present to one's life.

Even distractions, or especially distractions, that take one's attention out of one's fleshy self contribute to disembodiment. Distraction can be a coping or defense mechanism to not feel what's too painful and fearful. Disembodiment is basically the condition of one's not "being fully present in one's body." This happens rather frequently for most of us, even though we may not recognize it. Where are your feet at this moment? Do you find yourself looking down, looking for them as if to look for a nearby object? Do you attend to and really notice things in your environment when you go through your day, rushing from one place to another, from one task to another?

Typically, our attention is constantly called out of our selves, and kept away from our selves. Contemporary childhood seems to be particularly prone to this disembodying and dissociative condition as children are more and more subjected to the constant attention-grabbing practiced by the external world of parenting, schooling, media, lateral socialization, consumerism, and so on. There is literally an attention war being waged on the battlefield of each child's consciousness. I am not aware of a disembodiment scale test (that is based on my understanding of disembodiment here), but I would be very interested to know the extent of disembodiment amongst today's youth.

When I look back at those twelve years of intensely competitive schooling, with the constant and unremitting pressure to perform academically and succeed, I would say that I could not have attended to my feeling matrix in any generous or deep way. My attention must have been tied up a lot with meeting externally imposed high-stakes demands, such as endless tests and exams. I was not deeply in touch with myself. The first Socratic injunction is "Know Thyself." This to me is the central and foundational aim of education. Hence, all the practices we impose on students in the name of education, but that are conducive to their disembodiment, negate education. It is mis-education. From this understanding, I wonder how much of what goes on in schooling is really mis-education. I invite readers to reflect on and examine their own schooling experience without feeling put on the defensive.

Return the attention to where it belongs: to the fleshy organism of the self! That, to me, is an urgent educational goal. Learning to be embodied means rehabilitating one's attention to the organism and its matrix of the felt sense. In practical terms, this rehabilitation requires that the organism be supported in certain aspects. I would characterize this support in terms of protection, repair, restoration, and resourcing. (I learned these terms in my study of body-based psychotherapy.) Basically, any time an organism is overwhelmed by stimulation overload from shock, trauma, wounding, and/or undue demands, it tends to go into disembodiment. It loses touch with its own force field of subtle and dynamic energy, sensations and feelings. This is part of the legacy of our physical survival mechanism: under stress, the bubble of subtle feelings and sensations bursts, releasing us to instantaneously flee, fight, or freeze in paralysis, mental or physical.

One of the greatest learning activities that I have been engaging in for the past two decades is meditation. Meditation is an activity (even though it may take the form of sitting still) of getting in touch with sensate and mostly non-discursive interiority. Hence meditation is an embodiment practice. While different people may meditate for different reasons other than embodiment, I meditate to return my attention to its origin: to the organic sensate life-force field that surrounds *this* being, right *here*. I am following the Socratic program of education: Know Thyself. To know myself, I must be present to the sensate, energetic life-force field that is my being.

LEARNING TO CONNECT

This little chapter won't be complete without my sharing one of the most challenging types of learning that's going on in my life right now: learning to connect. In recent years, I have been reading a lot in neuroscience, especially about neurobiology as explained by Daniel Siegel (2010). Also watching Jill Bolte Taylor's *My Stroke of Insight* (Taylor, 2006) TED Talk left a huge impact on me. As well, I have been reading Iain McGilchrist's *The Master and his Emissary* (McGilchrist, 2009). What all these scientists are pointing out is that the human being is basically a two-brained animal. Two brains—left and right hemispheres—joined by a wide, flat bundle of neural fibres called the corpus callosum, are packed into one skull. Each brain experiences reality differently and specializes in different functions.

Among many differences, what interests me the most in my present learning is that the right brain specializes in perceiving the embodied world of body language, emotional expression, context, implicit meaning, holism, and connection, whereas the left brain specializes in abstraction, analysis, denotative language, the mental power of manipulation, and categorization. With the left, we see the world in the conceptual clarity of sharp distinctions and categorizations, which is abstract and emotionless; with the right, we see the world in a warm and hazy glow of everything somehow connected to everything else and meaningful. Obviously we need both brains working hard for us to be successful in living, but the difficulty that we have created for ourselves in the modern world is that it prioritizes and prizes left-brain function over right-brain function. What does it all mean for me or for you? Let me talk about myself, and I will leave it to you to reflect on yourself.

I can plainly see, when I look back at my own education, that my left-brain development far exceeded my right-brain development, in keeping with the orientation of modern civilization. My 12-year schooling in Korea and 10-year schooling in Canada both strongly supported me to become a highly developed analytic, conceptual, discursive, problem-solving thinker, communicator, and academic writer. Lest I be misunderstood, I clarify: I am not condemning and complaining about my left-brain development. I am grateful that I had a first-rate opportunity for that, and glad that I am doing the kind of work that I do. The concern is over what was lacking or underdeveloped (see Cohen's chapter in this volume). Of course, in the way of learning, it is never too late to learn something valuable. Remedial learning is due.

Ironically, I have been in the position of teaching what I wish I had learned earlier. (Perhaps the meaning of "ironically" here is that this is how this wonderful universe of ours mysteriously works.) Eighteen years of professorship has been my absolute best opportunity to learn, with and from my students (and, of course, my two children and my husband—my toughest personal "Zen masters"), what I didn't get to learn or learned only superficially during my own two decades of schooling. I had an "Aha!" moment realizing that the research topics that interested me and continue to interest me have to do with right-brain matters! To wit: how to see the world as alive, intrinsically worthy, sacred, and beautiful; how to act with kindness and compassion; how to be more empathic and intersubjective; how to *just be* with another human being, not falling constantly for the impulse to control, direct, shape, and solve problems; how to rest in beingness, without cogitation and agitation; how to realize the interdependence of all things and honour relationality; and so on. And most of all, I am learning the toughest lesson of loving boundlessly and immeasurably. Failures and mistakes abound in my learning.

These matters of the right brain that I am trying to learn cannot be approached simply or predominantly through the left-brain ways that I excel in. Has anyone succeeded in connecting with and loving another human being through arguing and debating? I grew up seeing my brilliant mother (who never went to school) outwitting everyone through her skills of verbal argument; I went for my Honours BA degree in Philosophy that was all about analysis and argumentation; I did my doctorate in Philosophy of Education. Again, I am not debating or criticizing the merit, power, and usefulness of my training. I have been handsomely rewarded for my training. But it is what is underdeveloped that I'm concerned about. My education was one-sided, literally. It privileged and prioritized the left side: the left brain that specialized in the brilliance of discursivity.

How many times, even in the last few days, have I caught myself arguing my way into trying to connect with people, especially my loved ones? A totally self-defeating approach! Unless we are talking about purely instrumental connection with people, connection here requires emotional attunement and resonance. Discursivity has little to do with such connection. Allow me to illustrate this: Suppose that your child comes to you in distress. She is upset and crying. The distress has discursive content, for sure: for example, being socially ostracized in school. What's your first response? If your first response is to suggest how she/we can solve that particular problem, then you are not connecting with your child. You have not emotionally attuned to and established a resonance with your child. You may have suggested the most brilliant plan for solving her problem, but it is not likely that your child will smile and say, "Oh, thank you! I now feel much better." If this were one of my girls (brilliantly perceptive and articulate), she might have said, "Look, Mom, are you a machine or what? I am emotionally hurt, and your response is about solving my problem? It's not helpful! I want to know that you are *with* me!"

A couple of years ago, I was taking some counselling psychology courses. In my Counselling Skills course, I was role-playing a counsellor with my peer who played a client. She presented to me her troubling issue. The issue had to do with her job satisfaction and feeling caught between worries about financial security and unhappiness in doing what she does not enjoy. There were some other life issues that were part of her anguish.

My professor was emphatic: our job as a counsellor was not to solve clients' problems but to first and foremost listen to them deeply and emotionally connect with them. And yet, there I was, unconsciously falling right into the habit of problem solving and starting to tell my client what she could do to address her issues. In our counselling courses, we were reminded again and again that the cornerstone of counselling and psychotherapy is establishing an emotionally safe, supportive, and trusting counsellor-client relationship. Only then is the concrete work of helping our clients possible. I think educators need to be educated for the same understanding. Establishing a human relationship must happen before we can work with our students over whatever knowledge, information, and skills they are to learn.

It is not that there are no problems to solve and issues to address. The world and our personal lives are full of them. We have to wonder, though, how many of our problems and issues have sprung up precisely because of our inability to emotionally connect, and because we approach the world predominantly through the left brain. If many of our problems in the world fundamentally have to do with our lack of empathic understanding, kindness and compassion, acceptance of and respect for the other, then we must teach, alongside critical thinking and problem solving, how to foster and increase our capacity and ability to connect, attune, and resonate. And let me emphasize: such teaching must not be didactic and discursive, if it is not to be self-defeating and useless. But this also brings up the issue of how to undo the unconscious habits that keep us doing the same things again and again producing the same results we don't like or want. This brings me back to meditation or contemplative practices, and to pedagogy that is psychologically astute and attuned, all of which, in my view, need to be an integral part of education in all educational settings.

In the previous narrative, I said that I meditated for embodiment. In the present narrative, I will say that I meditate to develop witness consciousness. Both embodiment and witness consciousness are inseparable aspects of human beings' holistic, integrated consciousness. The witness consciousness has the ability to "see," be aware, and reflect on what's happening in the moment in the consciousness. For example, suppose I am livid with anger, and am about to explode, verbally or even physically. If my witness consciousness is sufficiently developed, and kicks in at the moment that I am about to explode, I may have an instant "stop" experience. I see, in my "mind's eye," what I am doing and what I am about to do. This awareness brings me to a pause. It is like someone inside me pushing the "pause" button. This "action" may be sufficient to discharge the energy—locked up in anger manifest in the moment—and I may be brought down into a calmer state. In this calmer state, I can reflect, assess, evaluate, and maybe even plan a different choice of response and course of action.

If I am quite advanced—I'm working on it—in my cultivation of the witness consciousness, I might not even go all the way to a state of near explosion. I would be in constant touch with the vast ocean of my felt senses, and see what's happening there long before any of the subtle and dynamically shifting feelings could gather a charge and storm up onto the surface in manifest and active emotional forms, such as anger, hatred, frustration, envy, jealousy, greed, and so on. It is a very hopeful thought, to an educator like me, that the human consciousness can be cultivated to this degree, in the service of creating a more harmonious and flourishing life for all.

REFERENCES

De Waal, F. (2005). *Our inner ape*. New York, NY: Riverhead Books.
McGilchrist, I. (2010). *The master and his emissary: The divided brain and the making of the western world*. New Haven, CT: Yale University Press.
Siegel, D. (2010). *Mindsight: The new science of personal transformation*. New York, NY: Bantam Books.
Taylor, J. B. (2006). *My stroke of insight: A brain scientist's personal journey*. New York, NY: Viking Penguin.
Yagelski, R. P. (2009). A thousand writers writing: Seeking change through the radical practice of writing as a way of being. *English Education, 42*(1). Retrieved from http://www.nwp.org/cs/public/download/nwp_file/13969/A_Thousand_Writers_Writing.pdf?x-r=pcfile_d

CARL LEGGO

LEARNING POETICALLY

hat does it mean to become a teacher? What does it mean to become a learner?

CARL LEGGO

REMEMBERING SCHOOL

The Heart's Haunting

Life is a sorry tailor.
(Bloch, 2006, p. 22)

Again I can almost remember.
(Buechner, 1999, p. 89)

I can change the story. I am the story.
(Winterson, 2001, p. 5)

The truth about stories is that that's all we are.
(King, 2003, p. 2)

My first granddaughter Madeleine will begin school in September. I am both thrilled and fearful. I am happy that she is looking forward to Kindergarten, to new adventures, to attending the school where her grandmother has been an Educational Assistant for a decade. But, at the same time, I am full of fear that school will not adequately support Madeleine's learning journeys. I have been a student or teacher all my life. My life has been devoted to schools. For fifty-five years I have "gone to school." I know schools intimately, and I know why I am full of fear. The fears I have for Madeleine are the same fears I experienced when my daughter Anna and my son Aaron began school. My fears were often confirmed in the many stories they lived in many schools in four provinces of Canada. What kind of wisdom do we need for learning to live well, with/in wellness? I need to write with love. My memories are fragments I turn and re-turn, seeking the heart of wisdom. But why are my memories stained, steeped even, in fear?

Spectres

I hold so many memories
even if I made them up

memories of elementary school,
hallowed and haunted

spectres, a spectral Spirograph,
circles in circles, gerbera daisies

in a greenhouse, no meadow,
all connected, all distinct

school, an alien place,
a planet where I wandered

with a plan, a treasure map,
A instead of X

a carefully plotted series of A's
with the promise of treasure

When I was young, my parents burned coal in the little house on Lynch's Lane. Old Man Giles delivered coal in a horse-drawn sleigh. The horse gasped and snorted, and its breath rose up like light smoke from its dilated nostrils. Old Man Giles removed the hatch in the side of the house, and shovelled the coal from his sleigh into the basement of the house. Later the sun shone through cracks in the hatch door, and lines of coal dust filled the air. My memories of Lynch's Lane are motes of dust in a beam of light. Sometimes when Old Man Giles wasn't looking, Cec, Frazer, Macky, my brother, and I sneaked rides on his sleigh, especially along Dove's Road on our way home from the Salvation Army Academy. We grabbed an edge of the sleigh, leaned back on our heels, and raced over the snow. Really we didn't go very fast, actually not a lot faster than we walked, but I always conjured up more in my imagination. Old Man Giles probably knew we were hanging on, and let us stay a while before he turned, and said *shoo shoo shoo*, in a whisper that sounded just like the sleigh in snow, and I was never sure if he was telling us to get off the sleigh or just humming with winter's echoes. Cec and Macky sometimes grabbed the bumper on ESSO trucks and pretended they were water-skiing. Sometimes they went really fast. I was never brave enough. I liked fictional adventures. They were safer, less fearful, more readily controlled and contained.

Carol Gilligan (2002) claims that "it is difficult for young boys to read the world around them and show the sensitive, soft sides of themselves" (p. 63). I am not sure what difficulties I experienced as a young boy, growing up in a working-class neighbourhood in a mill town in insular Newfoundland. I remember being a boisterous, competitive boy who loved sports and games of all kinds. I was physically active, seemingly tireless, full of boundless energy. But I also remember that I was always watching others, seeking to discern motivation and emotion, hoping to translate the stories I witnessed. Gilligan notes that "boys at around the age of five, if they are to become one of the boys, must conceal those parts of themselves that are not considered to be manly or heroic" (p. 91). I do not remember much trouble with my being "one of the boys," but I can recall many incidents when I was not especially brave or risk-taking. I was afraid of crazed bullies, loud extroverts, and grinning liars (I still am afraid!). I was afraid of the dark and I was afraid of pressing crowds. A few years ago, Tommy, whom I have known since Kindergarten, recalled how we once waited for Santa Claus to arrive at the train station. While waiting, I lost my family, and with a surge of panic I began running around, probably crying, shouting for help. I had long forgotten the incident, but Tommy will never forget. I can recall many experiences of fear that suggest I was not a rough and tumble kind of boy. I have likely concealed many parts of myself. I did not fit "cultural codes of masculinity" (Gilligan, p. 91), but I likely did not fit any cultural codes. I was athletic, imaginative, academic, sensitive, conscientious, intuitive, intelligent, energetic, diligent, motivated, curious, and questioning. I could go on, but the list already sounds self-serving and inordinately self-congratulatory. And I have always borne a reluctance to promote myself. As a boy I was not in touch with my emotions, with my intuitive understanding of experiences, with my heart's hunches and longings. As Gilligan understands, "there is no way to love freely, to experience freedom in loving, when you cannot feel your feelings" (p. 71). As a child I felt my feelings, but only some of the feelings. I knew anger and fear, but I did not know love. Now that I am old, I am beginning to review the long journey of six decades on the planet, and I am beginning to view plainly how the boy is always close to the man. As Wendell Berry (1998) knows: "The young man leaps, and lands/on an old man's legs" (p. 169). I am now constantly surprised by the daily stark lesson that I have gotten so much wrong in my life. No wonder I am full of fear for my granddaughter Madeleine as she begins school.

In her novel *The PowerBook*, Jeanette Winterson (2001) recommends: "Break the narrative. Refuse all the stories that have been told so far ..., and try to tell the story differently" (pp. 62–63). This is what I need to do in my storying. Winterson also writes that "history is a collection of found objects washed up through time" (p. 286). In my life writing and poetry I have surrendered any anticipation that I can tell a complete story, or even a coherent story. Instead my stories emerge as mosaics of coloured glass or fragments that catch the light or evoke memories or hold traces of sensory experiences that might have been or might be. Winterson (2001) reminds me that "there are so many lives packed into one" (p. 119), and that "the one life we think we know is only the window that is open on the screen" (pp. 119–120). There are always other stories, other possibilities, other windows.

With a commitment to other possibilities, I offer stories, poems, ruminations, quotations, and photos like windows opening up, closing, sliding on the screen. I offer a few photos from childhood as a performance of images for conjuring stories—invented, reflected, refracted, reframed. As King (2003) understands, "what the camera allows you to do is to invent, to create. That's really what photographs are. Not records of moments, but rather imaginative acts" (p. 42). And, in the way of imagination, photographs invite stories, interpretive possibilities for attending to writing in light. And I include my poems, in part as exemplars to illustrate my discussion, but also as performative texts that interrupt the flow of my expository writing in order to prevent a seemingly seamless texture that masks the tensile and tension-filled weaving of multiple texts and contexts.

WHEN I SPEAK OF LEARNING, WHY DOES FEAR TAUNT AND HAUNT ME SO?

Life then and life now have no connection,
or merely one in melancholy.
Things are all sealed up in pastness,
helplessly, and don't look out,
or if so then only falsely.
(Bloch, 2006, p. 62)

How have the stories of my school experiences shaped me as a teacher and learner? When I was graduating from high school, I submitted the following motto to be inserted below my yearbook photo: *Work, Worry, Win!* I think I thought I was being clever, playing on the alliteration of words beginning with *W* like I had re-invented the 3Rs. I haven't paid much attention to the motto, but now I see the words as eerily prescient. Today is a national holiday in Canada, a sunny Monday without commitments. I still woke up at 6:30 am (without an alarm clock), stirred psyllium into pineapple juice, grabbed a banana, and sat at the computer to work. I might have gone for a walk, or sat on the patio with a book of poems, or purchased a few more songs from iTunes, or curled up in silent stillness with prayers, ruminations, and meditations. Instead, here I am, working. And worrying about whether I will meet the deadline for this paper. (Why can't we have livinglines?) And worrying about what I said at the last department meeting, or what I didn't say. And worrying about students and colleagues, publications and citations, grants and awards, merit and the morality of just desserts. *Worry* is derived from the Old English *wyrgan*, to *strangle*. I am strangled with worries like a neurotic, compulsive, obsessive worrywart! My school graduating motto is a noose around my neck, a ligature around my heart.

In school I memorized facts, countless scientific, historical, geographical, mathematical, literary, and grammatical facts. I tucked them away on index cards in drawers in my memory. Today, the only fact I can recall is that John Cabot discovered Newfoundland in 1497. Today, I know the fact is not true. Newfoundland had long long ago been discovered by the indigenous people who called themselves the People, the Beothuk. All those facts I learned were really fictions, made up stuff for explaining the world in particular ways, often manipulative ways for constraining understanding and behaviour.

The motto *Work, Worry, Win!* still strangles me. There is so much I want to learn. I want to learn about absurdism, Botox, carpentry, dodoes, electricity, Facebook, GarageBand, holograms, iMovie, jihad, Kabbalism, love, Michel de Montaigne, Nicaraguans, opossums, photography, Qatar, reality, sagacity, televangelists, ukuleles, Viogniers, wackos, xanthomas, Yakimas, and Zarathustrians, but I am afraid to try, afraid of failure, afraid I will waste my time.

CARL LEGGO

Chopsticks
(for Erika)

all my adult life
   (a long time)
I have been
   a teacher

and for almost
   six decades
I have been
   a learner

some years ago
   I wanted
to learn how
   to use chopsticks

living in a city
   more Asian than Caucasian
I felt disrespectful
   asking for a fork

school taught me
   well the fear
of trying, a dangling
   gold star, my goad

till, one day,
   with precise
gentle instructions
   Erika showed me

suddenly I could
   pick up sushi
sashimi tempura
   California rolls

with an invitation
   learning swept
in with delight
   dispelling fear

I will lean
   into learning
sense and senses
   breath and blood

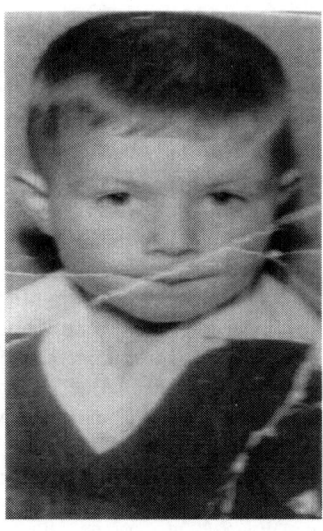

Figure 1

WHEN I SPEAK OF LEARNING, WHY DOES FEAR TAUNT AND HAUNT ME SO?

How do we ever know who we are?
(Bloch, 2006, p. 27)

Of course, there is a big difference between learning how to use chopsticks and learning how to love, or learning how to be a Papa, or learning how to be happy, but in my life story, learning skills and facts is definitely related to engaging with the curriculum of becoming human. I learned fear in school, especially the fear of failure, the fear of not excelling, the fear of missing the mark. I learned to avoid risks, and stick close to what I knew well. I learned to memorize and repeat like a prattling parrot. I learned to offer polite smiles without wiles, to keep my opinions, beliefs, and hopes tucked away in secret compartments. Now I know that the heart of learning and teaching requires passion, creativity, and imagination. Skills and facts have a place in learning and teaching, but they are not the heart of education. I have spent my life in schools, and everything I say about learning and teaching is refracted through my experiences, and those experiences might not be reliable or compelling. But what I know, I know refracted through the lenses of experience. And now, those experiences seem remarkable only for their narrow limitations.

My father was an electrician. I do not remember ever asking him to tell me anything about his work and knowledge. My father-in-law is a carpenter. Years ago, he helped me build a couple bookcases. I remembered those bookcases recently. I remembered how I used a chisel to cut the precise lines for inserting the shelves, and how I selected a precut moulding to trim the bookcases, and carefully painted them with an enamel-based cream like French vanilla. I never built anything again. Nevertheless, a few years ago, my father-in-law sent me a gift of money at Christmas. I went to Canadian Tire and bought a workbench where I store tools and screws and nails. I don't expect to use the workbench, but it reminds me of my father and my father-in-law, and of possibilities for learning that I missed or neglected or rejected, especially because I was devoted to the fallacious and fraudulent and flatulent promise: *Work, Worry, Win!*

My learning has been too much driven by the competitive fantasy of winning. I was the ideal student in school because I enthusiastically embraced the ideological orders of my teachers like an obedient soldier. I learned to goose-step and march and salute with an automaton's obeisance to programming and instruction and rules. I have written carefully in the lines, and I have been written carefully in the lines.

In grade seven I was a Boy Scout. I tied knots, made crafts, memorized *God Save the Queen*. I was a good Boy Scout. I imbibed Baron Robert Baden-Powell's wisdom like I was a British soldier in India, even if I was a 12-year-old boy in Newfoundland. With a Christian background I have leaned faithfully on the Apostle Paul's summons: "Do you not know that in a race all the runners run, but only one gets the prize? Run in such a way as to get the prize" (1 Corinthians 9:24, NIV). Now, the Apostle Paul wrote a lot of untenable, disputatious advice, or at least many people have been misinterpreting him for a couple millennia. It is difficult to know what Paul really wrote and said. And it probably doesn't matter all that much. What is important for me in the present is the way that I imbibed the Apostle Paul's advice like a challenge and moral for writing a life, my life, others' lives.

Horseshoes

on a long slow commute
down Boundary Road
I read the tattered sign
   Want to learn
   to pitch horseshoes?
   Wednesday 5-7
I've never had a desire
to learn to pitch
   horseshoes
and if I had a free Wednesday
I doubt I would
   want to spend it
with people who
pitch horseshoes
   but still there is
     something
about an early summer evening
and pitching horseshoes
high and long in an arc

from one stake to another,
knowing that pitching
horseshoes, like checkers,
is a mostly useless game,
neither physical nor cognitive
like running or chess,
   an old man's game
to pass an hour or so,
a few hours one doesn't feel
any need to hold fast
   in a miserly way,
just hours like pennies
you are happy to let go
     (what do I know about
     pitching horseshoes?)
and perhaps my father
   had more wisdom
   to share with me
   than I ever knew
if only I had learned
to listen now and then
like horseshoes imitating
pigeons from stake to stake
back and forth with as much
meaning as any of it makes

Figure 2

CARL LEGGO

WHEN I SPEAK OF LEARNING, WHY DOES FEAR TAUNT AND HAUNT ME SO?

This is my story. But it is not my story only.
(Miller, 2005, p. 176)

My memories of school know no end. Perhaps teachers felt the need to hold fast to the forms and guidelines, structures and strictures, of standardized curriculum objectives that could be evaluated with overtly objective obduracy. Schools were impersonal. Students did not know their teachers and teachers only knew their students in particular ways, the ways of unruly subjects that needed rules and ruling. I remember the line-ups, the marking, the folded hands, the arms held high in the air, the regimented discipline. I remember well the whoosh and slap and sting, bite and horror and hatred of each flash of the strap, whether it was my pink palm or another's. Only now, an old man wondering when I will get the senior's discount at the Bay, am I finally seeking the unruly subjects, the subjects that deny the rules, the ruler, the rule, the measured rule, the straight ruler, the marks and demarcation of the ruler. I have finally grown unruly, truly but ruefully unruly.

James Hillman (1999) reminds me that "living a long life serves soul-making by bringing to life the psyche's amazing collection of adjectives" (p. 11). I like Hillman's notion of a collection of adjectives, and I could list many modifiers that might catch glimpses of the boy I was and the man I am becoming, the man I have been becoming for a long time. But I am especially intrigued by Hillman's notion that "character is characters; our nature is a plural complexity, a multiphasic polysemous weave, a bundle, a tangle, a sleeve" (p. 32). When I look back at images of myself as a boy, when I remember stories of myself as a boy, I am mostly impressed by how the boy I was remains implicated and complicated in the man I am. There are so many characters narrating the stories of the character of Carl, a character in a lifetime of stories. So, as I write about the past, and write about emotions and experiences, I know that what I write is neither descriptive nor definitive. What I write is creative and tentative. I am exploring the past in order to acknowledge my connections, my historical and autobiographical kinship with many people in many places. I am not writing in order to "know myself," but in order to know that I am mostly unknowable. And while that might seem like a pessimistic or even hopeless enterprise akin to writing myself into a scholarly corner with no doorways to new adventures, I actually understand the process to be eminently hopeful and imaginative. I am not staked to the identities of my past stories. I have been a character, many characters, in many stories. I have been inscribed, likely indelibly, by those stories, but, like Hillman, I also understand that "life review is really nothing other than rewriting—or writing for the first time—the story of your life, or writing your life into stories" (p. 91). Hillman promotes stories as the way we create patterns and art and understanding in the flux and flow of daily lived experiences (p. 91).

I am still the boy I was. I am still fearful, afraid of hurting and disappointing others, afraid of hearing my parents' complaint that I whine too much. I am still the boy I was. I still long for a parent's touch, a parent's explicit word of love. But that boy has learned strategies for living with fear and longing, and those strategies are the ways of writing and poetry and creativity. As Hillman reminds me, "forgetting, that marvel of the old mind, may actually be the truest form of forgiveness, and a blessing" (p. 93). I live with the blessing of forgetting, but in order to forget, I must first remember. I live in the littoral spaces of sea and seashore, walking amidst the tides, the ebb and flow, always searching, always seeking a sure-footed balance that cannot be taken for granted. Like Hillman, I am "correcting course all day long: This is the beginning of wisdom. It is a practice, a quiet noticing of where you actually are, not of being right on, but of being slightly off" (p. 128).

Recently I saw another motto: *Love, Laugh, Live*. My third granddaughter Gwenoviere is a year old. She laughs all the time. Yesterday she was wearing a T-shirt with the slogan, *I Love Papa*. Of course, I laughed loudly too. Imagine if my yearbook motto had been: *Love, Laugh, Live*. Delightful alliteration! Strong wisdom! I might have composed a different life story with a different motto. Of course, I don't know what would have happened in school if I was devoted to love, laughter, and living! Sounds dangerous!

Smiley

at fifty-nine
I have finally
   caught up
with the smiling face
of the 70s iconic,
   perhaps ironic,
certainly ubiquitous
wide-eyed Greek
comic mask, once
long ago, pinned
to my bedroom wall

the mask first born
in 1953, my year too

I am happy
   I am having a nice day

when young,
Lana asked me
   often
if I would ever
be happy

   after years
of grumpy responses

CARL LEGGO

she stopped asking

now I am old
with enough aches
& brokenness
to remind me
    constantly
my biological
& chronological
    sixty is just
around the corner

& knowing so
many who had
    no chance
to turn the corner

I am happy
    I am having a nice day

like a tightrope walk
on the braided threads
of the heart's light
I walk the curriculum
    of delight
with a precarious poise
between emotions
    & emoticons
Forrest Gump's muddy face
& Wal-Mart's sales job

conscious
    conscientious
even conscientized

by pop culture's
facile philosophy
without a conscience
to sell me anything
I will sell myself
    for

I am happy
    I am having a nice day

LEARNING POETICALLY

one more testimony
to the ineffable
   efficaciousness
of poetry for spelling
the messy mystery
of living & loving
in this spell-bound
   earth-bound world
   beyond words

Figure 3

WHEN I SPEAK OF LEARNING, WHY DOES FEAR TAUNT AND HAUNT ME SO?

*From the past, it is my childhood
which fascinates me most .... I read
quite openly the dark underside of myself.*
(Barthes, 1977, p. 22)

My grade seven teacher died recently. On the web site for Fillatre's Funeral Homes I saw an image of Mr. Chaulk. I don't remember ever thinking Mr. Chaulk was an apt name for a teacher, but then I really don't remember thinking whimsical or witty thoughts in elementary school. Indeed, I don't remember many humorous or imaginative moments in elementary school. But it is also likely that what I call my memories of elementary school aren't really my memories at all. They might be memories of stories I was told. They might be memories of stories long forgotten, or mostly misconstrued, an amnesiac's wild meanderings. Recently I invited students in a graduate class focused on creativity and communication to write about sensual memories of elementary school. I have engaged in this kind of remembering and writing on many occasions in the past, and sometimes I think I have exhausted all I can recall about elementary school. But I was surprised as I wrote with my students, surprised as I deliberately focused on all the elementary school teachers I could remember. The first teacher I recalled vividly was Miss Hicks, my Grade 4 teacher. I attended the same school from Kindergarten to Grade 8, and I could remember each teacher from Miss Hicks to Mrs. White in Grade 8. I remembered them with the kind of vivid recall a person might enjoy with rear-view binoculars. Each teacher practically stood up and waved! And as I remembered them, I was surprised by how much I remembered them with fondness. I remembered strict Mrs. Thomas who still smiled most of the time, and Mrs. White who always seemed tired and vulnerable under a mask of cheerfulness. As I remembered my elementary school teachers, I was struck by how often my memories are simply not accurate. The memories might be false, or falsified, or calcified, or sanitized, or fictionalized, perhaps supersized like a heart-threatening hamburger. And that is why I need to interrogate all my memories, attitudes, practices, beliefs, and views. I need to bring an ironic curiosity to all my learning, and speaking of learning. I am still in process, still learning, still leaning on the past like a pediment, but more and more recognizing the past might be an impediment to my learning. Of course, if it is an impediment, it is not one I can ignore or escape. I might learn to lean on the past with a keen commitment to new interpretations.

Fire

in the Sahara-dry summer,
heat like a dusty musty rug,
everyone on Lynch's Lane wheezing
asthmatically in the peasoup
mustard peanut butter air,
houses exploded

God's judgment, Armageddon
on the doorstep, announced Uncle Esau;
spontaneous combustion, heat build-up,
boasted Dale, grade ten chemist;
arson, bad luck, evil spirits,
arsin' around, revenge, smoking in bed,

mumbled/whispered/wheezed others:
and only I knew though I couldn't tell

after Mugs O'Reilly's big boarding house
burned for twelve hours, the firemen left
a black rubble and I wished
I'd never hidden in the tall elm
outside Bonnie Lee's window
hoping to see her undress

Buck Cunningham's house hooked
into the side of a rock burned
and Buck like a baby crying
and running around in his underwear
telling the firemen what to do,
and I wished I'd never hidden
in the tall grass and discussed
with the boys what it would be like
to do it with Bonnie Lee and I
wasn't even sure what doing it was

and Maisie Shepherd's house burned
and I wished I'd never stared at ladies'
underwear on clotheslines, looked
at *True Detective* and *Stag* in Tom's store
when Tom wasn't looking, stood under the
iron stairway to look up Miss Robson's
dress, gave Eddy Mosher my recess money
to draw pictures of naked women, once
watched Jed and Pikey play strip poker
with Jan and Holly in the shack of spruce
boughs and cardboard deep in the woods

and I was Shadrach, Meshach, and Abednego
walking through fire a pyromaniac
in an asbestos suit firing the world

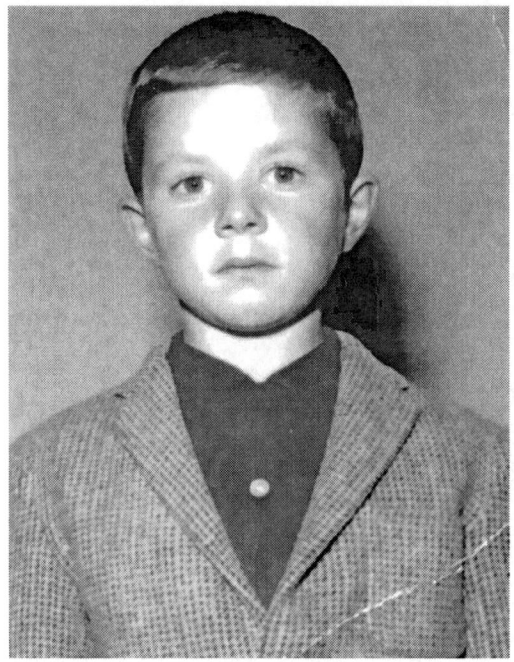

Figure 4

WHEN I SPEAK OF LEARNING, WHY DOES FEAR TAUNT AND HAUNT ME SO?

*The stories are maps. Maps of journeys that
have been made and might have been made.
A Marco Polo route through territory real and imagined.*
(Winterson, 2001, p. 63)

As a boy I composed a newspaper with my brother. We had a little printing set with letters etched in rubber and an ink pad that always left our fingers stained. We laboriously composed the text and printed it and sold the paper to our mother. I always remember the advertisement, *Brush your teeth with Pepsodent and you'll wonder where your teeth went*. My brother and I laughed a lot as we composed our newspapers.

But I don't remember ever writing anything in school that I liked or laughed about. I recall I once wrote JUNK in block letters on the paper cover of one of my textbooks. The teacher asked me if I really meant it, and I said, *No, not really*. I liked being a scholarly student, but I was a serious young man who could not understand much of what was going on. Did I ever write about anything important? At least important to me? I don't think so.

Later, in high school I wrote a speech for a competition sponsored by the Lions or Rotary, perhaps both. I wrote about pornography. Why? Why was I concerned about pornography as pollution? I don't know. I was like a demented teen TV evangelist with both wacky aesthetics and wackier ethics. I didn't win. Did I ever write poetry as a boy? Did I know any poets? I remember in high school really liking Karl Shapiro's "Auto Wreck" and asking an actor who visited the school to read the poem. I liked the sounds of words. I spent so much time worrying about handwriting with a cursive flow and knowing the correct answers even if the questions weren't worth asking. I spent so much time worrying about tidiness and cleanliness, stepping stones to godliness, even though I don't remember thinking much about God. I don't recall ever writing about experiences that were important to me in my personal life. There was no place for autobiographical writing in school. I don't think there was much place for the personal. Were my teachers frightened by the daily lived and living experiences of students? Perhaps my teachers were frightened by me, by the unknown. I had so much enthusiasm as a child. Now that I know the etymology of "enthusiasm" is "possessed by a god," I can acknowledge that I was possessed by wonder and creativity. I was enlivened by questions and ideas. But I learned to tame the wildness, to pretend a kind of conservative obeisance. It has taken many years of learning to unlearn the stories of military-like duty. (I must not forget that I spent the first nine years of school in a place called the Salvation Army Academy!)

Apple Cider Vinegar

As a boy, I didn't smoke in the henhouse
with Terry and Jerry, didn't play strip poker
with Jan and Jed, Holly and Pikey
in our shed of spruce poles and cardboard
deep in the woods near the Indian steps
rising in the rock cliff to heaven
or at least to Old Man Way's house.
And that was something else I didn't do:
call the old man the Old Man.

I learned catechism for Sunday School,
tied knots for Boy Scouts,
memorized English Kings
so my brain would grow,
and when Dex said he'd replace
my broken hockey stick, I believed him.
I believed everything Dex said.

And I grew up with eyes burned blind
by darts of lightning,
innocence trapped in the scent

of garden roses, untouched thorns,
finally learned I have no talent for goodness

and wished I had stolen green apples
from Old Man Way's garden
with Terry, Jerry, Jan, Jed, Holly, Pikey, Dex,
eaten them in big bites of wild autumn cider,
expulsion from the garden inevitable
as the expiration of breath:
I can no more keep the garden
than I can swallow the moonlight.

Figure 5

WHEN I SPEAK OF LEARNING, WHY DOES FEAR TAUNT AND HAUNT ME SO?

> *Every trace of our days on earth*
> *is framed by an enormous night,*
> *backward as well as forward,*
> *individually and above all cosmically.*
> (Bloch, 2006, p. 148)

I write all the time about myself. I am an autobiographical writer. But do I really write about myself? Who am I? Who is the *I* in my writing? Have I ever met him? What happens when I speak about *him* with an unspoken understanding that I am really writing about me? Perhaps it is true that when I write about *I*, I am really writing about the *I* I want to be, or the *I* that will not be contained or revealed in a story or poem, the *I* that boasts or at least courts an epistemological and ontological identity that has never been named, never expects to be named, even refuses and refutes nomination, the noun's blind arrogance, convinced only that verbs pulsate and oscillate with creative agency.

I grew up in a working-class home where few photographs were taken. It was too expensive to pay for film and developing. So, the entire collection of photos from my childhood is approximately fifty images. This is the whole of a working-class family archive. Therefore, the school photos of elementary school are especially significant because they are a part of a small collection. I don't have photos of high school classes. Most of the photos are black and white, and most are blurry or faded. Nevertheless, when I look at the photos, I am struck by the still seriousness in so many of the images. Like Barthes (1977), I see in these images something irreducible in my childhood: "everything which is still in me, by fits and starts" is "in the child" (p. 22). Above all, I see fear in the face of the child in so many of the photos.

These images are apparently me, but it is not apparent that I am in these images. The images are not me; they do not capture a sense of my identity. Instead, I construct interpretive contexts around these images, these photos. I imagine the person who is hinted at in black and white, in scratchy colour, in the cast of shadow and light. I write stories to explain, to contain, to interpret the person whose life is cast in the photographs like handprints pressed in cement. In all my writing I am writing a story in the sand, in the snow, in the sky, in the air, in the ocean, in the imagination. Every story is an effort to make connections, but no story lasts, is lasting. All the stories are elastic, even arbitrary.

Aliens

in elementary school I chased Betty and Janet
in go-go boots like Nancy Sinatra wore
and nylons that crumpled around their knees
not knowing what I'd do if I ever caught them
once slipped into a storm sewer ditch spring swollen
Janet laughing as I tread water and tried to grin
once almost caught Betty but knocked her down
and broke her collar bone   for years
I was in love with Betty and Janet but I can't
remember their playing with Cec Frazer Macky
my brother and me   can't remember if they ever
tobogganed or built tunnels in the snow
or erected forts or joined our snowball battles
remember only the icy storm sewer ditch   Janet's
loud laugh   the tear of pain in Betty's face

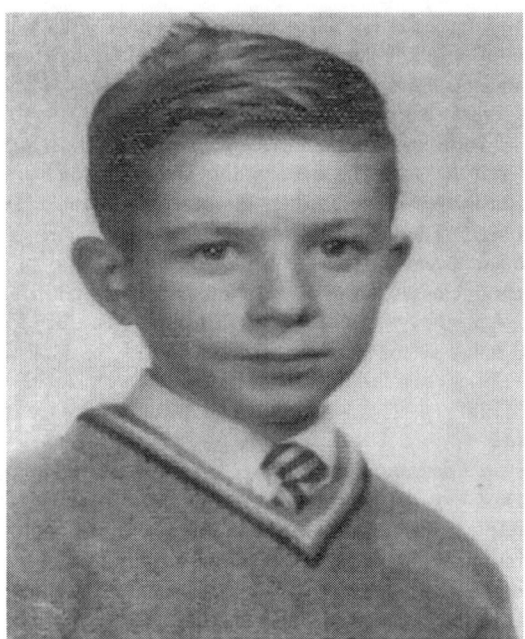

Figure 6

WHEN I SPEAK OF LEARNING, WHY DOES FEAR TAUNT AND HAUNT ME SO?

> *The mosaic of the past is a fragment—*
> *a bit of coloured glass, a corner of tile—*
> *but the present is no more complete.*
> *The paint is fresher, that's all.*
> (Winterson, 2001, p. 99)

As I look at the photos from the time I was a child, they trigger many memories. Are these memories real or accurate memories, or are they the memories that I constructed as stories of childhood based on evidences in the photos? My memories are resilient, perhaps far more lasting than I want to admit. But perhaps I am frightened by remembering, eager to live in the present moment, perhaps unable to live well in forgiveness, unable to accept that the past is always present, always a part of my life, not only like a part that precedes, that holds "in the beginning," that comprises the first sequence of chapters. Instead the past is still present. It is still being lived, or it is still alive, or it is still living. I want to say that the future does not count, has not yet been lived, and therefore does not enter into my storied universe. But, as a Christian, I believe in the future. While it is true that I often question and contest many Christian beliefs and theological arguments, especially conservative perspectives that are based on misinterpretation and hearsay, I am, nevertheless, a professing Christian, a Christian professor, and so, I am filled with hope, an eschatological anticipation for what is promised, what is still to unfold, what still remains to be revealed. The future is then like the past, also present. Perhaps the future is the telling of the stories that are possible when we attend to the art and heart of story-telling. Perhaps the future is the panoply of versions of stories that can be told to reveal the world. "Future" is a "word." So, I am not talking about linear progress—I am talking about growth to freedom, growth in spirit, a keen sense of artful attending in the momentous moment.

In his short fiction "Funes the Memorious," Jorge Luis Borges (1998) writes that Funes "thought that by the hour of his death he would not even have finished classifying all the memories of his childhood" (p. 323). Like Funes, I remember a lot, but I am even more interested in all I forget. Are remembering and forgetting like light and shadow in a photo, sound and silence in music, movement and stillness in dance?

Freddie

with his carrot red hair
and asthma and nose
like a leaky faucet
Freddie wasn't pretty,
a rusty crusty mess,
and in grade eight
a thousand times
a day he twisted
his head a perfect
180 degrees to see
Paula in the back
in her short skirt
that covered nothing, and
a few times I turned, too,
to check out the colour
of Paula's underwear,
and Paula always stared
back like she was counting,
and the room was always
hot and hard, and
I remember Mrs. White,
at the blackboard,
the back of her blouse,
a gap where a button
had been missed or burst,
a glimpse of cream skin
and a black bra strap,
and the air was filled

CARL LEGGO

with the pungent scent
of Dustbane used by the janitor
to keep the dust down

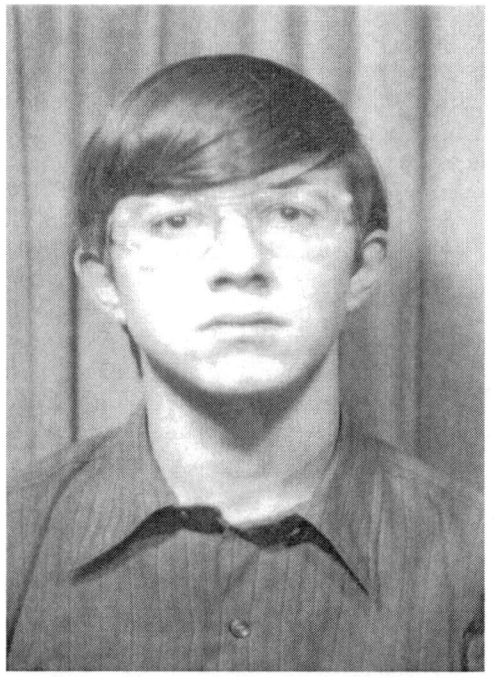

Figure 7

WHEN I SPEAK OF LEARNING, WHY DOES FEAR TAUNT AND HAUNT ME SO?

> *Writing is a way ... to open up*
> *the word and the world,*
> *and our lives within*
> *that world for attention,*
> *discussion, understanding,*
> *re-imagining and re-creating.*
> (Chambers, 1998, p. 26)

I have written many poems about growing up on Lynch's Lane in Corner Brook, Newfoundland. Recently I returned to the neighbourhood where I grew up, my first visit in several years. Almost everything has changed. Almost everybody I knew as a boy has died or moved. Many houses, including my parents' home, have been destroyed as part of an extensive urban redevelopment project. And, yet, in my memory's eye, I saw the old neighbourhood, vibrant and vivid and vital, almost as if I was watching a film. In my poetry I store the memories of family and neighbours; I record the stories of ordinary people, and I know the extraordinariness of their lives. I seek to honour the people I grew up with, even when the stories are hilarious or horrible. Above all, their stories haunt me, and I want to hallow their memories.

In *Pedagogy of the Heart*, published posthumously in 1997, Paulo Freire acknowledges from the perspective of a long life nearing its end that his childhood backyard was a space connected to many spaces "where this man of today sees the child of yesterday in himself and learns to see better what he had seen before" (p. 38). For Freire, "a posterior view of the world can be done in a more critical, less naïve, and more rigorous way" (p. 38). We all need to pay attention to our own backyards, the people and places that shape us. To write our own stories is to explore the heart with its rhythms and energies and emotions; to write our own stories is to communicate and connect with the stories and the hearts of others. I only wish I had learned to write these stories as a student in school. I was a graduate student in my thirties when I began writing the stories of growing up, the stories of memory. At least, once I started, I never stopped. Now, I know how all my writing is a part of an ongoing conversation without end, or any beginning I can recall. I am wandering in the wilderness of stories, swirling about in words I no longer seek to tame and ride like a broken horse. Now I breathe the wildness of words, ever ready to read my stories in new ways. I seek only a literacy that refuses the often oppressive authority of the literal. My pedagogy is not about finding or composing a way; my pedagogy is about being and becoming the way.

Battle

driven by Saturday western and war matinees
Cec, Frazer, Macky, my brother, and I
fought renegades, enemies, desperadoes,
built forts and camps and bomb shelters
in snow and scrap lumber and blankets,
and saved the world for God and democracy
and civilization in bloody vicious battles
(truces only for meals)
wielding wooden and Woolworth's guns
and sawed up broom handles for grenades
and snowballs melted to lethal iciness
and screams to curdle grandmother's blood,
but the real battle took place
on a June afternoon outside Penney's store
when Bobby Buckle, dark and mean
like a wolverine, threatened to rip
my nose and ears off if I didn't give him
my Mountain Dew and Cherry Blossom bar,

and I knew the hand grenades in my pockets
and the karate I'd practised on Cec
and even the cap pistol in my belt
weren't much good against Bobby Buckle
and I was swallowing a hard knob of fear
and the harder need to surrender
when Macky said, Shit off, Buckle,
and Bobby Buckle's eyes went from black
like licorice to black like onyx
filled with fire and his hands closed
into dense metal balls, silver and flaring,
and Macky, a pillar of rock, stared
at Bobby Buckle who glared and cursed,
but Macky didn't even blink his eyes,
and Bobby Buckle swung around like a cyclone,
missed Macky and continued spinning
all the way down Harbourview Road,
and I let Macky have the cherry
in my Cherry Blossom bar

WHEN I SPEAK OF LEARNING, WHY DOES FEAR TAUNT AND HAUNT ME SO?

> *Real life at school is ...*
> *not lived during classes*
> *but before and after them.*
> (Vargas Llosa, 1995, p. 53)

To remember is to "recall to mind," to once again "be mindful of." To remember is to learn to listen again, to see and hear and understand in new ways. In his autobiography Mark Twain (1990) wrote a familiar refrain about memory: "I am grown old and my memory is not as active as it used to be" (p. 4). He then adds that when he was younger, he could remember anything, "whether it had happened or not" (p. 4). With winsome wit, he adds that his "faculties are decaying now and soon I shall be so I cannot remember any but the things that never happened" (p. 4). I probably shouldn't trust my memories, but they are like guideposts on the journey that keep me oriented. I am haunted by my schooling. I have many more stories to tell, many more stories to remember, many more stories to hold fast in the light as I continue to interpret and translate the many experiences that have shaped me along the way, in ways I know and do not know. And as I continue to write and interrogate my memories, I will focus on what I know in order to remind myself to keep transforming what I know into what I do not know. In other words, I most want to face the fears that taunt and haunt me so I can live with reverence and hope for possibilities, always learning how to learn, always learning how to teach.

Salvation Army Academy

I remember
        kindergarten, the first day,
        crying, dressed in a white shirt

I remember
        report cards, school photos
        being glad my textbooks were new

I remember
        egg salad sandwiches wrapped
        in wax paper in brown paper bags

I remember
        the boys' washroom
        piss and antiseptic

I remember
        Sadie Jenkins who everybody said
        never ever took a bath

I remember
        the beam of dust seen when the sun
        peeked through the hole in the blind

I remember
        Miss Hicks who smiled and seldom got angry
        the prettiest teacher I ever knew

I remember
        swinging in the alder trees, spring and autumn
        bursting in rough buds of light

I remember
        the strap sitting on the teacher's shoulder
        like a limp tongue

I remember
        the smell of a new leather briefcase,
        how we'd take turns sticking our noses in

I remember
        punching Glen in the stomach because
        he said he had really hard abs—he did

I remember
>day-dreaming about
>kissing Janet

I remember
>the poster with a line of gold stars
>my own Hollywood Walk of Fame

I remember
>bells, shouts, angry voices, bells and more bells,
>like the principal's voice full of threats

I remember
>aqua ink in Sheaffer fountain pens
>no ballpoints allowed

I remember grade 8
>when I memorized so many facts
>I had little room left for anything else

I remember
>thinking that adults were odd,
>hoping I never had to become one

And now at 59 years of age, with a lifetime devoted to learning and teaching, I know adults are indeed odd, and I know I am one, but the child I once was in elementary school continues to haunt this now older man's heart. Like Winterson (2001), I now understand how "explanations drain away. Life is what it really is—a jumble, a chance, the upturned room of a madman" (p. 286). And with this acknowledgement, I am learning to lean into fear, seeking to hear the fear-mongering at the heart of so much of my learning so I can begin to linger in the possibilities of new ways of knowing and being and becoming. Always seeking to learn to live well, with/in wellness.

REFERENCES

1 Corinthians 9:24, New International Version.
Barthes, R. (1977). *Roland Barthes* (R. Howard, Trans.). Berkeley, CA: U of California Press.
Berry, W. (1998). *Timbered choir*. New York, NY: Counterpoint.
Bloch, E. (2006). *Traces* (A. A. Nassar, Trans.). Stanford, CA: Stanford University Press.
Borges, J. L. (1998). Funes the memorious. In J. Rasula & S. McCaffery (Eds.), *Imagining language: An anthology* (pp. 320–324) (J. E. Irby, Trans.). Cambridge, MA: MIT Press.
Buechner, F. (1999). *The eyes of the heart: A memoir of the lost and found*. New York, NY: HarperCollins Publishers.
Chambers, C. (1998). Composition and composure. *Alberta English*, 36(2), 21–27.
Freire, P. (1997). *Pedagogy of the heart* (D. Macedo & A. Oliveira, Trans.). New York, NY: Continuum.

Gilligan, C. (2002). *The birth of pleasure*. New York, NY: Alfred A. Knopf.
Hillman, J. (1999). *The force of character and the lasting life*. New York, NY: Ballantine Books.
King, T. (2003). *The truth about stories: A native narrative*. Toronto, Canada: House of Anansi Press.
Miller, R. E. (2005). *Writing at the end of the world*. Pittsburgh, PA: University of Pittsburgh Press.
Twain, M. (1990). *The autobiography of Mark Twain*. (C. Neider, Ed.). New York, NY: HarperCollins.
Vargas Llosa, M. (1995). *A fish in the water: A memoir* (H. Lane, Trans.). New York, NY: Penguin Books.
Winterson, J. (2001). *The PowerBook*. Toronto, Canada: Vintage Canada.

MARION PORATH

THE COMPOSITION OF LEARNING

We learn by teaching, through teaching, and for teaching...

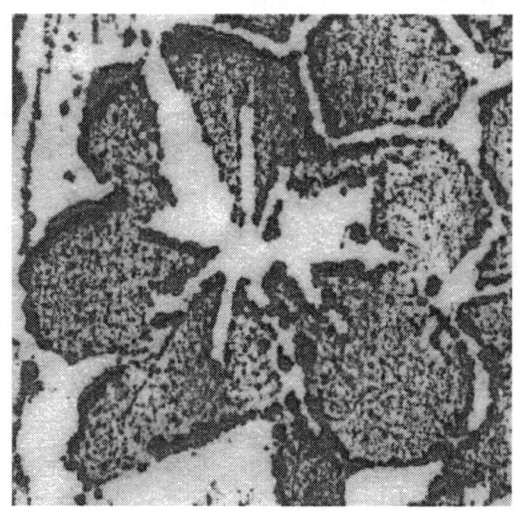

MARION PORATH

IMAGINING/IMAGING LEARNING

> *What is an artist? A provincial who finds himself somewhere between a physical reality and a metaphysical one .... It's this in-between that I'm calling a province, this frontier country between the tangible world and the intangible one—which is really the realm of the artist.* (Federico Fellini)

How is the intangible act of learning imagined and imaged? In this essay, I play with the notion of patterns in thinking about how learning has shaped my more tangible identity as an educator. My early learning experiences influenced my feelings about teaching as a career and, ultimately, my teaching philosophy. These early experiences also played a part in the development of my artistic self. My artistic identity developed more slowly but now I find myself drawn more and more to represent experience artistically through visual representations and writing in a more creative way than a long academic career often allowed. Here, I play with the notion of tessellations, images created through artful arrangements of shapes, to express my thoughts about learning. The word *tessellation* originates in art—the tiling and mosaics found in ancient cultures. Its etymology is Greek and Latin; tessella were the small cubes of stone used to craft patterns of intricate beauty.

Tessellations are a metaphor for the story of how my learning has unfolded and shaped me as an educator. Tessellated shapes intrigue me and provoke me to think about how I imagine my learning—the patterns that emerged over time to shape who I am as learner and teacher. When tessellated shapes are regular and repeated over and over, they form the rich patterns of mosaics and kaleidoscopes. To me, this periodicity reflects the foundational teaching/learning that results in mastery of facts and skills. While the teaching and learning may be straightforward—"regularly shaped" (teacher shows or tells; student practices and learns [Bruner, 1996]), what is learned can be integrated in complex, artistic ways, given time, opportunity, and sensitive teachers who are curious about who learners are and how they think. Each of us brings unique experiences and interpretations to our learning, provoking shifts in patterns made by "regular shapes."

But what if we start with the "irregular"? Begin with involvement with concepts? Tessellated art is more than patterns made from regular shapes, however beautiful those patterns may be. Deeply provocative are the tessellations created by the artist M. C. Escher using images from the natural world—stars, butterflies, shells, fish. These images were intended to move tessellations beyond graphical connections to conceptual connections (Schattschneider & Walker, 1977). They contain visual surprises. The viewer is "drawn to look again and again" to discover the imaginative world portrayed in the images. While still periodic in that the pattern that is the "fundamental cell" repeats in at least two directions and fits together without gaps or overlaps (www.tessellations.org), the conceptual emphasis creates the hidden surprises and provocations for which Escher is known. Like Rodari (1973), whose artful work with children provoked deep learning through imaginative exploration of the conceptual depth underlying words, conceptual tessellations provide imaginative ways of thinking about identity and experience.

Tessellations can also be aperiodic—semi-regular and nonrepetitive patterns that are not constrained to a defined space. They can go on forever, like learning paths that twist, turn, diverge, and build on each other continuously. They complement periodic arrangements of geometric and natural objects and reflect the myriad of ways in which learning happens.

PATTERNS

The word "pattern" has its roots in the early 15th century, meaning "model of behaviour, exemplar," from the Old French *patron* and Medieval Latin *patronus*. The use of "pattern" to refer to a decorative design was first recorded in the 1580s. Tessellations involve patterns—some repeating, others unique—but all reflecting parts of a whole. Bortoft (1996) wrote, "Because the whole is in some way reflected in the parts, it is to be encountered by going further into the parts instead of by standing back from them" (p. 6). Reflections of childhood memories of learning thus become seminal parts, or "fundamental cells," of an educator's being. The parts do not determine the whole, however. There is a "simultaneous, reciprocal relationship between part and whole, whereby the whole cannot appear until the part is recognized, but the part cannot be recognized as such without the whole" (Bortoft, 1996, p. 23). Learning is a patterned dance that never ceases. It continues to grow, reach, entwine, search for the light, blossom.

Figure 8

In childhood, I was in receptive mode. Bortoft (1996) contrasted this mode with the analytic mode that dominates human experience. The analytic mode is rational and sequential. Analysis certainly plays a major role in life as a scholar and educator but I strive to maintain the holistic and intuitive receptive mode (Bortoft, 1996) in my learning, allowing me to stay in the frontier country that Fellini described.

Identities of educator, artist, and researcher are intertwined in the work I now undertake (Irwin & de Cosson, 2004). These woven identities now reside in the in-between described by Fellini, providing a realm in which to explore learning. Engaging in this exploration coincides with my return to the place of my childhood, a successful professor of Education just retired, bookending in physical and metaphysical ways a life in which learning played, and continues to play, a significant role. I often drive by the school where I attended Grades 1 through 6. Margaret Jenkins School, the only school in Victoria to be named after a woman. It was, to a young child, an imposing structure—a tall brick building erected in 1914 (Victoria Heritage Foundation, 2009). It now has heritage status but the former expansive lawns and trees that gave it its colonial look are gone, replaced by modern appendages to the original brick edifice. It holds many memories. It is the somewhere between physical and metaphysical reality—the tangible beginnings of a career focused on teaching and learning and the intangibles of early thoughts and emotions that resonate with who I became.

BACKGROUND

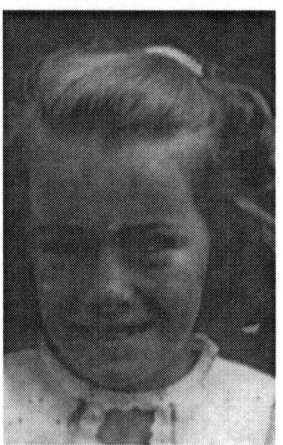

Figure 9

Red, yellow, and blue construction paper teddy bears.
Learning our primary colours.
Dick and Jane readers.

Math workbooks. Disconnected sums and take-aways.
Gold star rewards.
Regular shapes.
Children in rows.

In post-World War II schools, classes were large. I had no idea what the experience of school might entail. There was no kindergarten—no easing in to what school was about and what mattered. That first September, beginning Grade 1, I was confused by the ritual of lining up outside the huge brick building in the morning and after lunch, waiting for a whistle to be blown that signalled time to enter. I had to be rescued as I walked the unfamiliar halls looking for my classroom. There were 42 students in my Grade 1 class. Miss Haverstock, my diminutive white-haired teacher, was warm and welcoming, helping to ease the stress of so many new experiences. The noise of 42 six-year-olds was greeted with "Boys and girls, let's see if we can hear the pin drop." I remember the small silver straight pin that was used on these occasions and that sometimes someone actually did hear it drop, or claimed to. We behaved ourselves, as was expected by our teacher and our parents.

Figure 10

Order, rules, fill in the blanks, workbooks in a pile, the smell of paste (but not the taste—I was never one to eat paste like other kids did), desks in rows, fingernail inspection, clean handkerchief pinned to my dress. Routines, conventions, standards—noncreative tessellations mostly remembered as a blur of

MARION PORATH

expectations and little opportunity for individuality. These standards and expectations were important nonetheless. They provided a strong, dignified base from which to move forward. And, for me, there was a sense of belonging and satisfaction in what school had to offer.

There are vague memories of learning in my first year of school—mastery of reading, writing, and fundamental mathematics, being in the Robins reading group (what did that mean?), pasting craft projects on my oilcloth covered desk—but one memory stands out. I was writing a story. I remember the magic of words appearing on the page with very little effort and how the word "lovely" was one of them. I have no idea of the topic but my mind was often engaged with trying to capture in words and images the beauty of the landscape in which I lived. This story was an early experience of flow, a sense of deep happiness achieved in concentration (Csikszentmihalyi, 1990) on something I had figured out for myself and expressed to my satisfaction. I was also cognizant that I had read something subtle in the expression of another—Miss Haverstock was impressed, perhaps even a little shocked. Grade 1 classrooms in 1950 were places of one-syllable learning. See Spot run.

Figure 11

My final report card stated that I had "ranked first" in my class. I had no idea what this meant but it made my parents proud.

Fundamental cells ...
Serious
Engaged
Conscientious

Loving learning
Quiet observer.

Good little girl. My Grade 3 teacher, Miss Smith, liked me. I'm obedient and I'm smart. This was the good side of life in this classroom. I continued to do well academically and be engaged with learning.

Miss Smith explains the writing contest. Stories about Cinderella will be judged and the winner will receive a ticket to the Ice Capades. Suddenly I'm in another world, lost in the writing. The words flow onto the paper and I love it. I win! The world of Cinderella comes alive on ice. It is like I created it.

I was successful in this classroom but there's something sinister. Miss Smith tears strips off others who are less compliant, less able. She becomes another person with a twisted red face. I hate this. It gives me knots in my stomach and makes me feel responsible somehow. I feel the injustice. In my seat at the back of the class (I was always back there; gold stars and "ranking first" ironically result in back seat placements) I ache for those students who stumble in the round robin reading we do daily, increasingly anxious as my turn approaches. I'd already rehearsed over and over, having counted up the paragraphs so I was sure which would be mine. I could read this Grade 3 basal reader easily, having already tackled *Little Women* by flashlight under the bedcovers, but I take nothing for granted.

How did this teach us how to read or create an atmosphere that valued reading? I was fortunate to have a mother who loved reading and told me that one day I would read the volumes by Dickens on our bookshelf at home, and a father who brought home sets of books for me. My parents gave me worlds that allowed me to overcome the sterile, disconnected paragraph reading at school. But I couldn't shake the pain I felt for those who struggled. The tension in this classroom was palpable.

Tessellated images may metamorphose into other images or transform into three dimensions. Escher's tessellation, *Reptiles*, (http://www.tessellations.org/tess-escher9.shtml) shows two-dimensional tessellated reptiles stepping out, becoming three-dimensional, and exploring the three-dimensional world they had previously inhabited in patterned flatness. In my third year of school, I began to step out of the pattern, crawl over it, observe it, feel it, and question it.

Observe quietly.
Learn what people do.
Speculate why.
Learn how things are done.
The expectations, the outcomes, the joy, the pain.

Metamorphosis begun.

Now I realize that "quiet observer" is part of the pattern that informs my learning and teaching. This "fundamental cell" affords opportunities to watch and learn; it is how I learn best. Combined with empathy, it also allows me to feel the tone of groups, understand subtle signs of emotion, interpret body language, and recognize contextual factors that affect others. Current work on empathy (Baron-Cohen, 2011) allows me to determine that my "Empathy Quotient" (EQ) is very high. At age 8, a high EQ was likely part of who I was. Then I could do nothing. Years later, I put my empathic abilities, knowledge of my students, and a commitment to make curriculum meaningful and exciting to work to create environments for joyful learning. My students told me my classes were safe places to explore ideas and new ways of thinking and representing their knowledge.

The flow of writing happened rarely in school but the joy of it stayed with me and waited. It was the same with art. There was little instruction in or exposure to visual art at school, apart from crafts and seasonal cards that followed a formula. Memories are of "colouring in" or "colouring around"—careful blue pencil crayon edges fanned out evenly and exactly around maps of the British Isles, North America, Australia. Still, there was something wonderful about the colours, the techniques, the act of engagement with mark making. These formed the foundational pattern for a love of art. My class sketched a live model in Grade 3 but I was the model. I didn't learn much apart from how to sit very still in one position (perhaps I was chosen because of my ability to sit quietly) but the activity made me aware that there is an art form called still life that is challenging to render for the artist and hard work for the model.

There was no fine art displayed in my elementary school but my father's hobby was repainting rooms with each season's new colour and being bold about it ("shrimp pink" for the kitchen; chocolate brown and chartreuse for the living room!). Dad's enthusiasm gave me a colour vocabulary. Mom surrounded us with art and music. My cousin was an artist, a brilliant one whose representations amazed me. A latent love of visual art resided in me. Down to Rescue Bay—roses, sunshine, garter snakes on the path, tide pools, the rhythm of the ocean.

> Sketching at the beach
> Magical red-roofed lighthouse
> Light sparkling on the waves
> Vibrant tide pools
> Joy in the act of searching for ways to represent beauty.

Figure 12

MIDDLE GROUND

Fast forward. Dropped into the last months of Grade 6 in a new community. My teacher was an artist. She gave me skills and inspiration, made me feel like an artist too. I experienced flow again as colours came alive on the page, giving shape to a dramatic scene. "I would love to work with you," Mrs. Everall said. "It's too bad I'm moving away." I so wanted her to stay so I could learn how to make the block prints made by older students that were displayed in the hallway. I loved the look of them. How were they accomplished?

Grade 7. No more art. The shrill presence of Mrs. Duncan. There is a lesson on homonyms with a homework assignment to bring a list of 20 homonym pairs to school the following day. I bring 20. I'm not too moved by this homework but others are. They bring long lists to school. Mrs. Duncan melts down. She shrieks at me, wondering why, since I'm so capable, I haven't risen to the occasion. What's the matter with me? I feel the pain of public humiliation and a deep sense of being wronged. I did what was asked. Hidden agenda, inappropriate reaction on her part; profound distrust on mine. She repeats her criticism on my report card. My parents say nothing, apart from congratulating me on good grades. Lesson number one, Mrs. Duncan. Do not humiliate. Know your students and try to understand them. Be honest about your expectations.

Grade 8. A new teacher but Mrs. Duncan teaches us Math. She calls me to her desk to tell me I will go to university; I'm ahead of the others in the Math curriculum. She presents me with a book on algebra to study on my own. I had no idea what this meant. What, really, was I supposed to do with this book? I remember taking it home and looking at the first few pages. What was algebra and why was it important? Where was the context? Lesson number two, Mrs. Duncan. Explain yourself. Students need to know why.

At the same time she gave me the algebra book, Mrs. Duncan pronounced, "You'll be a teacher." "Oh no," I thought. "Not if you say so." To be like her would be the worst possible fate. Follow up on lessons number one and two—find out the future that students envision for themselves. Teachers can shape their practice, reflect, learn from how they experienced school, learn from their students. Experiences and study taught me this. But my adolescent self saw only the black and white—I will never be like you.

High school mirrored the experiences of my childhood. I loved learning and, in general, loved school. I continued to be encouraged to write and to attend university but no one was specific about the career I should pursue. There was no time or opportunity to follow artistic inclinations. I continued to be the quiet observer. This was criticized by my Grade 11 English teacher who asked why, when I could write so eloquently, I didn't say anything in class. Only I knew that there was considerable thinking going on. I also felt deeply that it was unjust to penalize someone for shyness.

> I am teaching Grade 4. Lori's mother comes to thank me for supporting her daughter to speak in class. It is the first time she has spoken in school—ever. I wasn't aware of this but sensed her sensitivity and quiet presence in all we

did as a class. Perhaps quiet observers recognize each other and take comfort in that recognition.

Undergraduate study consisted of quietly taking in course material, ways of teaching, and others' way of being in class and out. After two years, I floundered. Academics sustained me but other aspects of life impinged. I took five years out.

FOREGROUND

Back to school. Teacher education. I had no burning desire or well-developed rationale for taking this path but my ability to feel when things are right was reliable. I went on to dwell in the phenomenon of teaching and learning. It is part of human experience and shapes each of us in unique and varied ways. In the end, I overcame my resolve to prove Mrs. Duncan wrong and became a teacher. I knew there was a better and more fulfilling way. The learning of childhood, both positive and negative, shaped me as an educator.

The verb "learn" comes from Old English *leornian,* the meaning of which includes being "cultivated." The figurative meaning of "cultivate"—improving by education—is over 300 years old. Cultivation is a tessellated concept involving learning and teaching. One can make efforts to become "cultivated"; individuals can also engage in cultivating others. Growing, reaching, entwining, searching for the light, blossoming—all are related to cultivation. My teaching experience—11 years as an elementary teacher and close to 25 as a professor of education—cultivated my intertwined identities of educator, artist, and researcher.

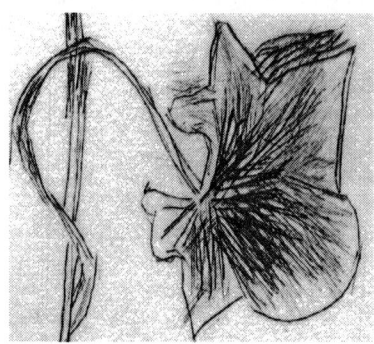

Figure 13

With just two years' experience, I prepared to teach thirty-five 9-year-olds. Many had what we now describe as "special needs." The pain I experienced as an 8-year-old from witnessing the humiliation of students who struggled came back to me and I sought to find ways into understanding my students' learning paths and reasons for acting out. These wonderful children made me laugh, cry, tear my hair in frustration, soar with pride. They are the students I remember best.

THE COMPOSITION OF LEARNING

I remember—

Thirty-five children in smocks, brayers in hand, preparing to ink their string prints. Total focus. Not one mishap. Sheer joy when they produced their prints.

Thirty-five children sitting up straight, hands on desks, quiet as I entered the classroom after morning recess. Why, I wondered. This never happened. Some catastrophe usually prevailed. Today the principal was in the room, preparing to do the required observation of my teaching. After he left, I thanked the children for behaving so respectfully. "We did it for you."

Coming back from a three-day absence due to sickness. "If you didn't come back today, Mrs. Porath, we were going on strike!"

Children's competence, capacity, love of art, ability to understand fine art no matter their background, joy in my joy in art, curiosity, efforts to understand and create are patterned in me, entwined in me. Add my curiosity about why things "work" and how children may have been thinking about the task at hand when things don't work; my need to excite students and be as excited as a teacher; and the need for all of us to grow as learners. In my work as a professor, I continued to develop the intertwined identities of educator, artist, and researcher/wonderer. Adult students' capacity, joy, curiosity, and ways of understanding were added to the pattern. The tessellations are more complex now but are built on the foundation of who I am and what I experienced in my early years of learning. Past and present learning tessellate. Patterns emerge, repeat, connect, transform, and blend in many ways, resulting in designs that weave narratives of learning into identities of teacher, learner, artist.

Rotation, reflection, superimposition, symmetries, asymmetries, metamorphoses ...

Figure 14

REFERENCES

Baron-Cohen, S. (2011). *Zero degrees of empathy: A new theory of human cruelty and kindness.* London, UK: Penguin Books.
Bortoft, H. (1996). *The wholeness of nature: Goethe's way toward a science of conscious participation in nature.* Hudson, NY: Lindisfarne Press.
Bruner, J. S. (1996). *The culture of education.* Cambridge, MA: Harvard University Press.
Csikszentmihalyi, M. (1990). *Flow: The psychology of optimal experience.* New York, NY: Harper & Row.
Irwin, R. L., & De Cosson, A. (Eds.) (2004). *A/r/tography: Rendering self through arts-based living inquiry.* Vancouver, Canada: Pacific Educational Press.
Porath, M. (2012). Developing the artistry of teaching. In A. Cohen, M. Porath, A. Clarke, H. Bai, C. Leggo, & K. Meyer, *Speaking of teaching ... Inclinations, inspirations, and innerworkings* (pp. 41–49). Rotterdam, The Netherlands: Sense.
Rodari, G. (1973). *The grammar of fantasy: An introduction to the art of inventing stories.* New York, NY: Teachers & Writers Collaborative.
Schattschneider, D., & Walker, W. (1977). *M.C. Escher Kaleidocycles.* Petaluma, CA: Pomegranate Communications.
Victoria Heritage Foundation (2009). *This old house: Victoria's heritage neighbourhoods. Volume four: Fairfield, Gonzales, & Jubilee.* Author.

KAREN MEYER

PLAYING FIELDS

*hile pretending to be someone or somewhere else, here is not here, & the real world is made up...*

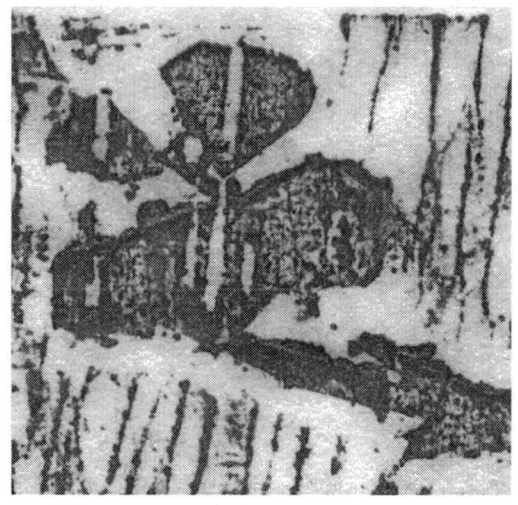

KAREN MEYER

FRIDAYS[6]

A Novel Memoir

1
two of us

اب made red paint on my hands disappear. Me and Wawa splashed in the kitchen sink till my pajamas felt soggy. My fingers turned wrinkly. Me and Wawa and finger paint made a big mess on the table. I squeezed the sponge and اب came out. اب likes to find holes. I made soapy train tracks on the table. اب likes to find me.

* * *

A few years back I found Wawa's journal in my father's basement. I was curious about the cardboard box labeled *Mom's Writing* sitting tight on a shelf. Bent corners and frayed edges let slip its age. It was taped shut. Opening the box felt like uncorking a vintage bottle of spirits.

When my curiosity got to the bottom of books and notebooks and loose manuscript pages, I spotted *Fridays with Shaya* handwritten on a Moleskine cover. Below the title, Wawa had taped a photo of the two of us sitting on a roller coaster seat, clasped hands in the air, her hair flying, me barely taller than the back of the seat and sporting an open mouth smile.

Page after page, my budding, skinny self leaped out in front of me. As I read her words, Wawa's voice, its intonations, as I remembered, took over the narration, recounting Friday after Friday. Fragments of boyhood lit up in my mind like scenes from a familiar film I hadn't seen in years. Each Friday episode in the journal belonged to Wawa and me, the characters. But the frayed, heirloom box labeled *Mom's Writing* and its cache of stowaway stories belonged to the entire cast of my family. I believe that was Wawa's intent, a gift to the lot of us.

You see, I come from wholehearted roots—unshakable roots, of the kind that hold a seedling, wobbly still, till it grows into its own being in its own time, whatever conditions. Extended family roots have advantages in childhood. Mine had backup systems, reinforcements, nets, which meant I didn't fall too hard, or too far from home. Some part of my raising from the ground up had to do with me spending every Friday with Wawa before I entered Kindergarten—those first few years when my child-self "joined the world," as Wawa put it.

---

[6] *Fridays: A Novel Memoir* is a fictional memoir about a man's memories of his grandmother.

Of course I was a fearless newbie back then, figuring out a whole reality of possibilities I needed to know in life. Learning for beginners requires becoming wired into the milliseconds of real time straightaway—in a world that has no time for a belated newcomer. In my case, I had to make sense of my world with binocular attention, between two languages and two cultures. Hard to tell apart one culture's looks, gestures, expressions, and expectations from another's so early in life.

Apart from that, I held the privileged position of being Wawa's first grandchild. My significant first learning experiences, waving a tiny hand, taking a step, climbing the jungle gym, belonged also to her as a new grandmother. The two of us underwent basic training, diving right into the many milestones of childhood. Mine. Even so, I turned up in last place among five older cousins on my mother's side, bound by birth order, inheriting their first-hand stories and their second-hand toys.

Wawa still worked as a university professor. She loved teaching. As far back as I can remember she stepped outside any box put in front of her whenever possible. She loved sharp pencils. She loved writing.

So did I. My Luke Skywalker shoes dangling way above the floor, I sat in her chair and wrote scribbles at her writing table (in both English and Farsi, though both looked the same). I remember it cluttered with books and notebooks and pencils with worn erasers. I loved erasing. At that table in her small apartment, I learned that reading and writing mattered to my life. Who would know this *mise en scène* was a snapshot of my destiny?

As Wawa's journal dates concur, in her busy life she rarely missed Friday with me. Nor did she miss writing about it. Her weekly entries documented the marvels of learning, the unfolding of my learning and her learning, and how to imagine learning differently.

My memory tells another story—what an elder means to a child's life. Wawa was mine. She followed in my footsteps, hardly ever stepping ahead. And she did so with a persistent patience. "And that has made all the difference." (Forgive my borrowing from Robert Frost.[7])

I had hoped my grandmother would follow my own son as he joined the world, like she accompanied my wobbly self down the road of childhood. I wished that one day the two of us writers would create something together across generations. But the gathering of my life to such a stage, father and writer, took some time for me. There were detours along the way.

Alas I have lost my childhood and lifelong friend. Still, we write this memoir together in spirit from an archive of Friday stories and, as you would expect, "outside the box" I inherited from Wawa. My memories of being three and Wawa's journal packed away in my father's basement go hand in hand, like Wawa and me loose on a Friday escapade by train, bus, ferry, or all three on occasion. We are two voices around a story. Two generations around a childhood. Mine.

---

[7] Frost (1916), "The Road Not Taken," line 20.

I admit my earliest memories I share here have materialized out of my 35-year-old imagination. But as a writer I stand behind my imaginary self, creative license and all. Wawa's journal about me back then was no doubt biased, maternal entitlement. She pronounced me the "perfect little Jedi" and the like on many a journal page.

That said, it's true that my grandmother showed up every Friday at my house. And I stood at the window Friday mornings waiting. I imagine me there like a cherub statue ready to come alive—lightsaber in hand.

The odd Friday I glance out the window next to my cluttered writing table, a cherub reflection looks back—smirk, pencil behind the ear, and I wonder where Wawa has gone off to.

Friday: Play Rules! (playing fields)

How I love my name! My given name. Wawa. Given to me by Shaya. Between he & I, Wawa means Play. A verb. An invitation. "Heh Wawa ...?" Shaya's my mentor. Tireless. Irrepressible. A Triple-belt Play Master. One belt earned for each year of his life. He invents Play. (In spite of all us adults around who've become incapable of true Play.) He lives it.

I believe Play is how Shaya befriends this absurd world—that he abruptly landed in—so it might become less strange. Less overwhelming. Shaya creates his own "playing field" of experiences every day. That's how he engages the given-ness & the mystery he encounters in his world.

I confess here that Play deserted my to-do list ~~years ago~~ decades ago. Rehab with Shaya means me relearning the subtleties & nuances of Play. Unplugging the dominant hardwiring of my left brain. But I'm not discouraged. It's been over two years of weekly practice with Shaya. I can play in full mode ~~all afternoon~~ for a few hours.

Shaya has three rules about Play. I learned them as: Imagination, Presence, and Openness (to be followed all at once, of course).

Imagination—Maybe the myth (??) that we don't use big parts of our brains is true in some way. Imagination requires loads of RANDOM ACCESS MIND (RAM). My RAM? Atrophied. I have memory leaks. When was the last time I imagined myself as an imaginary character, like a cat? Or imagined being in an imaginary place, like a soft billowy cloud? Not in my mind. Actually there. Can't remember.

Presence—This rule requires my entire attention. Awareness in the moment. Play moves at warp speed with hairpin turns. When I wander off task I miss the cues. Really, it's not that I have a short attention span (??). It's that my restless attention doesn't have a clue about how to be present anymore. About being-there.

Too much multitasking goes on in my life. Need to ask myself where I am now, now, now ...

<u>Openness</u>—*I've ditched any logic I've hoarded over the years. Doesn't work in Play. Here's how it really goes: Me & Shaya hide in the closet. Stay perfectly quiet. Except for giggles. There's no one else in the house. No one to come find us. Doesn't mean we aren't hiding. Make sense? So simple.*

NOTE: "Hiding & no seeking" is like a Zen koan (the sound of one hand clapping???). A koan is a paradox to show the inadequacy (and absurdity) of logical reasoning & to provoke enlightenment. That's where I'm headed. First I need to befriend the world. Create my own playing fields of experience.

2
real and pretend stories

Me and Wawa went to fire station. Me and the fireman fixed the hose. It was crooked. اب was stuck. I sat in real fire trucks, mine are pretend. Wawa telled the fireman to slide down the pole. Him wears a uniform. Him's real.

* * *

I learned straightaway in my new, inexperienced life that the proposition "ready or not, here I come" was not always a good idea. While running, even dicier. Either the world wasn't ready for me, or most likely, the other way around.

Ready or not, I was a Jedi once, and my family witnessed the entire foiled episode. Since I was only three, I take the never-ending story at their word, all four relentless versions. A single story kept inside my family—safe, sound, but ready to spill like beans—can have different protagonists, plots, points, pokes, and of course endings.

In defense of my Jedi character in the story, there was a second key factor worth mentioning here besides knowing if I was ready or not: knowing what was real and what was pretend, definitely a learned and discerning skill (based on both good and bad experiences).

Here's the story from my memory.

Everyone in the audience, including my mother and father, Papa and Wawa, are waving and smiling at me. That's me on the stage in the brown, floor-length Jedi hoodie with other kids twice my size. I've seen the photos. Just a moment before, I put my hand up like the other kids in the audience did, not knowing why, and a grown-up Jedi put on my hoodie, handed me a lightsaber, and escorted me away from my parents, Wawa, and Papa. I marched to the stage in a line of other Jedi characters in long brown hoodies.

On stage, the tall striking Jedi Master is no teacher. According to Wawa's version of the story, he is zeroed in on his lightsaber and being handsome. My little confused hand is tugging at the bottom of his robe as I follow his steps back and forth across the stage, almost tripping him several times. He calls out, "activate!" and the other kids extend their lightsabers, those cheap, plastic telescoping versions.

Now I could have stayed with the way things were going, even my faulty lightsaber not responding to "activate" and "de-activate" on cue. But music begins to blare out of giant speakers on the stage, the Darth Vader death march. This is a big Disneyland production after all.

My parents are still smiling and waving and taking photos. Can't see Wawa. Is this for real? Honest-to-God yes. Lord Vader himself stands on a platform rising from below the stage, tall, dark and evil with a REAL red lightsaber cutting through billowing smoke now smothering the stage. My blue plastic lightsaber is still deactivated.

Any logical reason to become utterly hysterical?

Any reason to be promptly removed from the stage (while the whole production goes on)?

My point: What *is* it with grown men in costumes?

Friday: The Art of Pretend

Shaya likes pretending to be a "nam." An impulse strikes him. He suddenly crawls on the floor. "Nams" in a high pitched little voice. When I don't catch on to the act, he prompts me like the director of a play (& still in his high nam voice). "Wawa, I'm a nam now." I respond. Scratch his head. Give him nam treats—Cheerios in a bowl. Dare I say on the floor??? Pull his soft, fluffy tail. He hides. Curls up on a pillow. Licks his paws. Assumes an aloof look. There's no costume. No props. I'm there to pretend along.

Why a cat? Why any particular moment? Don't know. Doesn't matter. It's art. Shaya's a performance artist. And no, I don't worry he'll still pretend to be a nam when he's 30. Though it could bring down the curtain on a dull, boring work meeting. Let out a quick "nam" instead of pretending to be interested in what's going on. It's all pretend in the end.

NOTE 1: While pretending to be someone or somewhere else, here is not here, & the real world is made up.
NOTE 2: "Nam" means cat. As a bilingual child, Shaya invents words in a third language of sounds for the benefit of Farsi & English speakers. Nam sounds like what a cat says. Brilliant.

Friday: Making Real

Shaya says to me, "Wawa, make it real." "It" would be one of his toys. I've learned how to speak for Dinosaur, Rainbow (his stuffed dolphin) & Superman as a character actor. Shaya speaks back as the protagonist. We create dreamed-up, make-believe situations, scenes, & stories. Improvise some highly avant-garde plots Shaya directs (lots of times in the bathtub).

*I believe "real" in Shaya's playing field means <u>seeing</u> inanimate characters "alive" & responsive. Like him. Why shouldn't Dinosaur, all 6 inches of plastic, be real **WHEN** it talks and walks (given what he thinks alive means)??? I'm not sure when this animated perception will end for Shaya??? Maybe when he assimilates the grown-up definition of "alive." That ends in foreclosure of any other possibility imaginable ... leaving only a figment of a talking dinosaur.*

3
welcome to my world of اب

I a Dolphin. Sometimes I a Nam-Dolphin. Nams live outside and in houses. Dolphins live in اب

* * *

In my early twenties, I got a tattoo of a Dolphin on the back of my right shoulder. The idea followed from my childhood, and I knew exactly the Haida design I always wanted. When I was three, Wawa ordained my animal spirit to be Dolphin. She told me I could choose another animal whenever I wanted, or another animal spirit might choose me. But as I grew up, Dolphin stayed with me as my loyal daemon, sharing its spirit of manna and breath at critical times.

I learned about other animals and their mystical characteristics when Wawa shared her animal medicine cards with me. The cards looked old. They stayed next to her bed, bound together by a black hairband, left on top of two books that explained each animal's story and qualities worth contemplating—creativity, patience, grace, generosity, transformation, and so on. Before I was able to read, Wawa told me the animal stories and their teachings from both Indigenous and Celtic traditions. I remember that both decks had the same animals with a few exceptions, my favourite four Celtic Dragons representing air, earth, fire and water.

Even as young as three, I knew the cards were special to Wawa, still she let me play with them on my own, making each one look even more used, adding bends at the corners. I would remove the band, spread the cards on the floor while looking for my Dolphin card, the most worn, and then I'd find the other animals in my family: Mountain Lion (Wawa), Hummingbird (Papa), Swan (Mother), Wolf (Father), and Dragonfly (Aunt). I'm sure I never put the cards away properly in the band and next to Wawa's bed, but none went missing in all those years.

I believe that my playfulness and my early, deep-rooted connection with اب cinched the choosing of Dolphin. اب and I go back as far as I can remember. Sinks, bathtubs, fountains, puddles, pools, water parks, ice cubes, rain, snow, boats, the beach. Wawa told me that when I was a fussy baby my parents held me near a sink or shower with running water and I became quiet and peaceful. اب was the first

Farsi word I learned, easier to pronounce than "water." Wawa didn't know many Farsi words, but she always used to say اب .

Friday: Playing Fields of اب

Shaya knows that what falls from the sky & a kitchen faucet is the same stuff as what's in a puddle, a pool & the sea. Clear or blue. Cold or hot. Flowing or frozen. An unmistakable sound in motion. Silent when still. اب *was one of Shaya's first concepts.*

When he was two, a sponge full of soapy water on his highchair tray held his attention longer than any of his toys. Or food for that matter. Squeezing, mopping up. Squeezing, mopping up.

Picture little Shaya standing on a chair. I'm turning the button on the kitchen faucet from stream to spray over & over. His little hands underneath. After a while اب *escapes to the floor.*

Now at almost four, Shaya swims. Submerges. Splashes. His whole body is a happy little dolphin at the pool.

Friday: In the Spirit of Learning

Following Shaya, I witness an agile, untethered spirit. Falls and gets back up dozens of times in a day as a matter of learning. At my age, I only think about staying on my feet.

Today the sidewalk ahead was icy. Shaya ran to skate and slide across with his Luke Skywalker shoes. He slipped. His whole body slid like a hockey puck. I heard a quick "I OK." We started walking again. He held my hand so I didn't fall & break. Like a fragile teacup.

4
wheels

Me and Wawa got a wagon. Wagon fits on the ferry and train. Sometimes I sleep in the wagon on the way home.

* * *

On Fridays Wawa and I took public transportation to get places, which turned out to be a significant part of our weekly adventures. As a result, my young self experienced a reality beyond my Saturday-to-Thursday world, as we ventured across the city—downtown, east side, west side neighbourhoods, and several train stations, ferry terminals and bus stops. Apparently, the day I was born Wawa made a commitment to not drive, claiming she wanted to be part of the solution rather than the problem of carbon exhaust poisoning the planet and her grandson. I lived a subway train, ferry and bus away from her apartment in the middle of the city. That's how she began and ended most of her Fridays with me.

At three, I felt I was too big to sit in the stroller. So, hats on and packs strapped to our backs, Wawa and I walked from bus stops and train stations to our destinations—fire stations, museums, parks, beaches, recreation centres, her apartment, and so on. And more than a few times, she carried the packs and me a short way at the end of the day. But as luck would have it, I inherited a luxury-size, previously owned green wagon in good shape from my older cousin. The wagon was a two-door convertible, good tread on the wheels, and storage cubbies under the front and back seats where we stashed our gear—a change of clothes, buckets and shovels, water bottle and lunch. It proved to be the perfect vehicle for us. We now had wheels. We had places to go.

Riding public buses, ferries, and trains during the middle of the day meant I encountered a mix of people, tourists, folks in wheelchairs, seniors, and those who, shall I say, functioned out of step with the rest of the world, but who on occasion smiled back when seeing my cool Oscar the Grouch hat and Spiderman backpack. Wawa took it upon herself to ensure I learn about and appreciate the rich diversity of people living in the city. When asked where I was headed in my green convertible wagon, I would say, "Downtown," and I still can picture that man on the street with his own shopping cart for wheels, who winked and nodded back.

By three, I did in fact know how to deal with tickets and lineups, acknowledge drivers, get on and off trains and buses, read numbers on buses, listen for stops, drop coins in a street musician's case, be both friendly and cautious around people. Sometimes elderly ladies didn't appreciate the front seats taken by wheels on the bus. Nothing that batted eyelashes and a smile couldn't fix.

Friday: Magic Ferries

It's the split second before the ferry doors open. Shaya, the shortest person by far in the crowd standing & facing the glass automatic doors, shouts, "Open sesame!" He knows all the cues. We opt for a front seat at the windows. Shaya stands on his seat. Makes his own horn sound seconds before the ship's horn blares. On the older ferry, there's a capped-off pipe near the window. He uses it to steer the ferry away from the large cargo ships in our path. We look for dolphins. Occasionally see a seal.

Shaya & I routinely take ferries, buses & trains. The trips are rarely routine. There's an unfolding plot on our way. Rather than a destination. The magic ferry is more than a means of getting somewhere. It prompts a narrative with real things & people. Shaya at the helm. Sure Shaya learns the rules of behaviour. Lining up. Taking a seat. But he also brings his rules of Play. Imagination. Presence. Openness. Shaya's playing field & the public world merge. A joint operation, far from figment & fantasy.

KAREN MEYER

Friday: Happiness is a Warm Lap

Today Shaya & I took the bus, ferry & train each way from the Science Centre. He fell asleep in my arms on the bus. The last leg home. The noise of a crowded bus on a busy street didn't faze him. He trusted the world completely. When he woke up in his bed, I'd gone home by then. I wonder how he remembered the day. I wonder how he experienced the day.

NOTE: Recently, I heard a lecture[8] about happiness & the distinction between one's Experiencing Self (ES) and one's Remembering Self (RS). Apparently, the two are quite different. We don't attend to the same things when we think <u>ABOUT</u> our life (RS) as when we actually <u>LIVE it</u> (ES). The ES deals with being happy <u>in</u> one's life & living in the present as continuous moments, one after the other. The RS deals with being happy <u>about</u> or <u>with</u> one's life, keeping score, maintaining the story of one's life. It's the storyteller; it makes our decisions. (We don't choose between experiences, but memories of experiences.) The researcher made the point that the ES should count more in our lives since how happy we are <u>with</u> our life doesn't tell us how happy we are living it. (One bad moment in a chain of positive experiences turns into a story with a bad ending.)

Shaya's teaching me how to attend to my ES. As he grows older, he may not remember our Friday escapes. Maybe only some stories. Maybe his remembering, reflective self is still developing at age 3. But his ES is full blown & learning happens.

5
forever an only child

> I got a baby brother at the hospital. Him cries a lot and sleeps in my old crib. My hugs make him stop crying. Sometimes.

* * *

The minute my brother was born, my whole life with only-child status vanished into the intense attention around a newborn. Playing by my gregarious self was not my strong suit. I still required at least a family audience for my gymnastic routines—my rehearsed jumps and rolls across the family room. But my parents were out due to sleep deprivation. The whole household had been abruptly taken over by a tiny person who couldn't walk, talk, smile, or do anything that could remotely be considered fun or entertaining. I never remembered being that dull, or that cute. Who does?

---

[8] Kahneman (2010), "The Riddle of Experience vs. Memory."

Wawa came to my rescue. I slept over Friday nights at her apartment more often. Her building had elevators. I could read all the numbers and reach her number five button. There was a police station across the street. I kept a close eye on police cars coming and going. Sometimes with lights and sirens on. When the trash truck made a commotion in the alley, I ran to the windows. That noisy gigantic truck resembled my toy model in colour and design. I loved trash trucks.

My bird's-eye view out the fifth-floor windows looked completely different from my home neighbourhood, with its houses, its maintained front and back yards. I could perch myself at those high-rise windows and watch the comings and goings of the inner city.

My grandfather was a professional musician. Wawa played drums. They devoted much of their small apartment space to musical instruments, a century-old upright grand piano, a full electronic drum kit, hand drums and various percussion pieces. My grandfather had a small studio space for his instruments and recording equipment. Papa allowed me to go into the studio when he was there. He let me turn knobs and strum his guitars.

Wawa bought me my first guitar, wooden with one string. It hung on the wall next to Papa's guitars. I owned my own hand drum trimmed with bright animal characters. When I played Wawa's drum kit, I couldn't reach the foot pedals, but I practiced making my way around the snare, tom-toms, cymbals and hi-hat at lightning speed. My drumsticks blurred with glitter.

Decades later, my brother, rather than I, became the musician of the family in our generation. Though I believe that small apartment, chock-full of opportunities to hear and play music, nurtured our appreciation for music.

Wawa kept some toys in her apartment for me, playdough, maps, superhero characters, but mostly we played with things I could find around the apartment, such as flashlights, shells, kitchen trinkets, art and writing supplies, which all required a practical imagination. Wawa kept a stepladder out so I could wash and play at the sinks, or climb on to her tall bed when it transformed into a train. As conductor, I made sure the train ran on time with Papa's compass for a pocket watch. Wawa and Papa always came on board as passengers. Wawa and I constructed tents all over the apartment out of sheets and clothespins.

At Wawa's apartment I was an only child again.

Friday: Playing Fields Forever

Some toys leave little to the imagination. Programmed to speak. Move. Give answers to predetermined questions. They over-prescribe a child's playing field. A voice goes off reciting the alphabet from the bottom of the toy box. Strange. Sometimes startling. Who pressed the button??? Even traditional, non-battery operated toys have newfangled designs. Shaya's baby rattle. A dead ringer for a purple cell phone. What's the point of that?

Playdough's still around. Tastes & smells the same. A few new colours. During our playdough time, Shaya rummages through my kitchen drawers—"Hmmm ...

what's this?" The garlic press. Potato masher. Devilled egg slicer. All speak to him, "What can we create with playdough?"

I've followed Shaya's development in the last two years from watching him play with playdough. Snakes & spaghetti aren't the only things he can make anymore. He creates cats with hats in boats. Pizza with yummy toppings. "Coming right up!" His little hands (& motor skills) are getting better at making what he imagines. Reminds me of learning to play a musical instrument. Time comes when your hands are able to play what's in your head.

Friday: Piano Notes

A piano lives in my apartment. The elder in the family. Made in 1901. I bought it when Shaya's father was 6 so he could begin lessons. I know nothing of its previous life. The formidable, grand upright, carved wood exterior has moved from city to city with us. The idea of leaving it behind??? Always vetoed in a family vote. So still front and centre in my small apartment. Still serves its noble purpose. Teaching big & little hands to play music. Like a wise master teacher.

When Shaya plays the piano, he likes to have a music book opened to a page. He says the notes look like trains going up and down across the page. There's an insight to his analogy. A connection between notation & higher & lower keys. Time we explore this connection. What else can we discover about "playing" notes???

Today Shaya was hiding toys. I was finding them around the apartment. He played piano keys, low & high, to indicate when I was hot or cold, near or far from the hidden dinosaur. Piano. A character in Shaya's playing field. Accompanied the game.

6
talking to trees

> Me and Wawa went to the park with trees. We talk to trees and know their names. I count ten trees name Pete. I ask Pete #3 for some moss for my ant house I build. Him said, "yes."

* * *

While Wawa and I spent much of our time together roaming the city, we also visited parks, looking for the ones with tall trees, her request, and challenging playground equipment, my preference. Wawa loved trees. We found the perfect park near my house with a natural landscape and paths that zigzagged through tall trees. I loved running fast down the grassy hill, doing my best not to tumble the way down. Wawa waited at the bottom every time, her hands covering her eyes.

She claimed she couldn't watch and that if I broke a leg she'd be in trouble. I would laugh all the way down. Later in my teenage years, whenever I went by that park I'd laugh out loud again, the thought of running down that grassy hill, it wasn't very steep after all. Things seem so much bigger and more dangerous when you're little.

I learned to talk to trees in this park. In truth it was Wawa's voice that answered for the trees. They were tall and hard to hear. Wawa seemed to know what they said when I asked them, in a polite manner, for a piece of bark or moss. They were generous those trees. Ants appeared to be moving all the time, one following the other on their way up and down the bark. I wondered if they ever rested. An even closer look inside tree bark revealed a network of bugs and sticky webs gripping ill-fated victims. A whole world lived and died inside bark. I learned that autumn was "spider web season," as Wawa explained. By age three, I was an expert on 'pider webs. I discovered you have to find "between spaces" to spot a web, the spider hides and watches off in a corner.

Wawa and I built ant houses under the trees (where ants could finally rest). We used moss, bark, sticks, rocks and leaves. I gathered the stuff and Wawa did the building, an opening for the door and a ring of rocks surrounding the structure. I have a photo, me kneeling beside our creation and pointing to the door. Sometimes when we returned to the park our ant house would still be standing.

I think any child can look at a playground and instantly size up the challenges and "fun factor." The playground at this park had climbing, hanging and spinning structures that tested my gymnastic skills. Wawa was never far behind me, ready to snag me when I was a stretch over my head.

Friday: It's the Small Things That Count

Today Shaya spotted a tiny, microscopic spider rappelling from the bottom of the TV. We got closer. Watched it make its way down the silk thread to the carpet. Four giant eyes on an oblivious, itsy bitsy guest. While we laughed it disappeared. Time & again, we reminded each other of that unexpected visitor. Laughed again & again. A spider coming out of a TV??? What next???

When I'm with Shaya, no event is too small or ordinary. The TV spider incident adds to our ongoing conversation about spiders & webs.

NOTE: When we've seen bigger spiders in the house we capture them and put them outside. The cup & cardboard trick.

Friday: Learning to Be Grandmother in Time

It's been a long time since I was a new mother. Being Grandmother serves a wholly different purpose. For the most part, parents lead children. Grandparents follow children. There's a different pace & a different relation to time & being-in-the-world. I've watched how parents walk with children. Fast. Forward. Future-oriented. On the way somewhere, school, lessons, and so on. This "hurry-up-time" shortcuts "lingering-time." Chances to dwell & dawdle in timeless activity ... Stomp in muddy puddles. Pick out the perfect rock from a pile. Poke at a bug to see if it's alive.

When I walk to the subway on my way to work I slip into hurry-up-time. Spend it. Beat it. Kill it in the rat race rush of "befores" & "afters." I forget that lingering time, authentic Now-Time even exists. I've become assimilated into clock time.

I follow Shaya along the exact path to the subway. We stop at the section of rocks under the bridge. Choose good ones to throw back. Walk on the abandoned train tracks. Push all the buttons at the station vending machine. Check for change. Go up and down the elevator. And eventually we get on the train & that's another whole experience. When we get seats at the front Shaya drives the train. He loves trains & elevators & rocks in his playing field. And we haven't even gotten to the ferryboat or the bus, or the Science Centre yet.

7
reading the signs

> Letters make sounds. I draw them at Wawa's table. Words talk. I don't hear them. Wawa teaches me to hear them. Wawa said that reading.

* * *

As long as I can remember, language has provoked my attention, particularly written language. Maybe that's why I finally became a writer. Growing up bilingual meant I had two first languages to learn at once, straightaway. That sounds quite daunting, but it was what it was. At three, I knew to turn my English books one way when my father read to me, turn my Farsi books the other way when my mother read to me. Fortunately picture books could tell a story in either language. What still fascinates me is how meaning, as slippery as it can be, emerges out of dissimilar utterances and alphabets.

My talking was slightly delayed, which is not unusual for bilingual children. In the meantime, I had developed a workable system of sign language and made-up words that sounded like an object (or animal). According to Wawa, I was captivated by signage, always asking her what a sign "said." She would patiently read them all, which amounted to a whole lot in train stations and ferry terminals, or at museums.

I owned a zillion children's books, and my parents read to me every night. When I graduated from afternoon naps to "quiet time" in my room, the adjustment was tough for me, I didn't think being quiet and alone was much fun. Wawa was sympathetic but reminded me that I could read books. I had great books. My reply was, "Wawa, I don't know how to read. I can only look at the pictures." It was true. Her immediate response was, "I can teach you how to read." She was a teacher after all.

Within a few weeks Wawa had gathered materials to start me on my way. Since I wasn't in school yet, she had the time to follow my lead, my interests, my timing. There was no hurry or need to struggle. We explored reading and writing together in some fairly non-conventional ways, for example, making giant letters and figures on her apartment floor with big plastic shapes that snapped together. We spent many hours at her writing table with fancy pens and sharp pencils I could choose. Erasing letters was as much a learning experience as writing them. Both my learning to read and my relationship to language unfolded at a slow and tender simmer with Wawa's patience.

Friday: A Time to Speak

It's humbling to watch Shaya learn to talk. Things change from week to week. New words. More grammar. Longer sentences. In two languages! I've started reading a bit about bilingual children. This experience is new for me. One theory makes sense to me. In a nutshell: when a child hears a single language, the brain "locks" on to that language fairly quickly. For a bilingual child, the brain has to stay "open" longer, so to speak. There's much more to learn. Shaya also has to know which language to speak with which grandmother. There's good news. There are advantages to this openness in development of the brain. More connections & skills flourish.

Then there's reading. Shaya's imagination has a new form to roam around in. The playing field opens up to fresh stories. Places. Times. I already see Shaya's readiness to read. He's curious about what words "say." (I hadn't noticed before how occupied the world is with written text.) He asks me to read signs, maps, menus, T-shirts, brochures, new books & so on. I read them. Point to each word when I can. It's only fair. Down the road, I'll be asking Shaya to read me a text too small for my eyes. Repeat words too faint for my ears. That I know will require great patience on his part.

Fridays: A Time to Listen

I loved my maternal grandparents. The elder characters in my family stories. At Shaya's age, I spent weekends at their tiny cabin. Followed Grampa around the property. Chatted at him too much (I'm told). Stamped out his cigarettes. "Helped" him rake the horseshoe pits & water the plant beds. He reminded me the tall trees didn't need watering, extended roots & all. Gramma taught me to bake biscuits. Make beds. Hang out clothes. She explained to me how to do these things correctly. I listened.

In my early 20s I logged many hours visiting my grandparents in their small apartment. They told me the old family stories. I told them stories about what I was up to. Both mattered. Grampa never finished school. We chatted about what I was studying at college over beer and tamales. He read a lot. Some days I came over with a life problem. I left with workable solutions. They never judged. They listened. I was grateful for their wisdom. Always.

When Shaya's a young adult I will listen to what he's up to. Maybe over beer & tamales. I'll want to hear stories about a world I can barely see & hear anymore. Let it be a peaceful world.

8
two of us (a handful of last words)

As an elder Wawa didn't have all the time in the world, but with me she acted as if she did. Let me say once more, it made all the difference.

I thought the world had taught me all I could possibly learn. Then Shaya came into my life. With utmost patience, he taught me how to wander about playing fields.

* * *

REFERENCES

Frost, R. (1916). *The road not taken.* Retrieved from http://www.bartleby.com/119/1.html

Kahneman, D. (2010, March). *Daniel Kahneman: The riddle of experience vs. memory* [Video file]. Retrieved from http://www.ted.com/talks/daniel_kahneman_the_riddle_of_experience_vs_memory.html

Figure 15

ANTHONY CLARKE

WHAT IF I HAD SAID "NO"?

M ilk, music, and memories ...

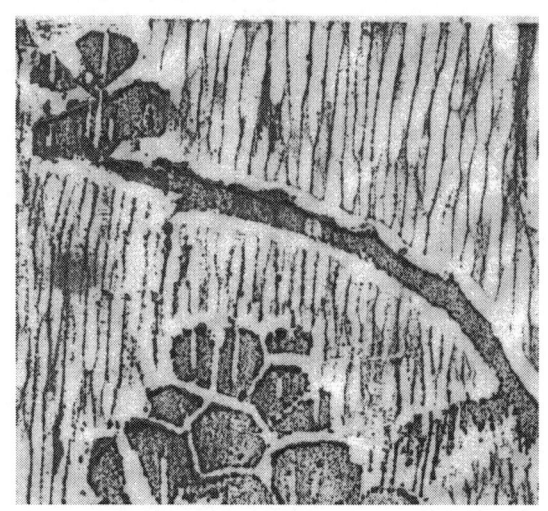

ANTHONY CLARKE

SPEAKING OF LEARNING

What Lara Taught Me

INTRODUCING LARA

The summer heat is both the beauty and challenge of living in Melbourne at the start of the school year. It is early February and the mercury is threatening to move into the high 30s for the third time this week. The holidays are over and we are into the first week of school at East Doncaster High School.

Figure 16

The bell sounds for morning recess as I chase the stragglers from my PE class out of the change rooms and back to the main school building. I follow my students into the lower quadrangle as I mentally rehearse the introduction of Nassi-Shneiderman diagrams for my Year 11 Computer Science class after recess.

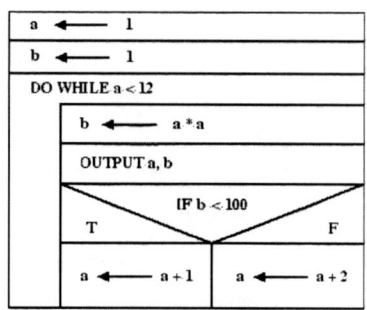

Figure 17

A shout interrupts my thoughts.

   Mr. Clarke. Mr. Clarke!

Amid the throng of students I see Lara hurrying towards me. I smile and before I get a chance to say anything she calls out:

   Are we going to enter?

I taught Lara three years ago in my Year 7 Physical Education and Year 7 Computer Studies classes but have not taught her since. She is slightly out of breath from her jog across the quadrangle.

Good morning Lara.

Good morning, Mr. Clarke. Did you hear about the contest?

What contest?

Big M on Triple M.

I shake my head as Lara continues.

First prize is a free Angels concert.

Lara and I are big Angels fans. We discovered this at the Year 7 Camp three years ago. Whenever we bump into each other now we exchange Angels stories. There are not too many things that we don't know about the Angels but she has caught me flat-footed this time.

Really?

We need to collect Big Ms.

Big Ms?

Yeah, it was on Triple M.

Big Ms on Triple M?

I feel as though I am in an echo chamber.

Yeah.

The bell rings signalling the start of the third period.

Lara, I have to get to class. Let's chat at lunchtime?

Where?

A-Block.

OK.

Lara turns and with a smile heads off to class. I have no idea what Lara is talking about. I have been away all summer and just returned to Melbourne. However, I do know that:

—Big M is Australia's most popular brand of flavoured milk;
—Triple M is Melbourne's most popular rock radio station; and
—the Angels are Australia's most popular rock band.

Figure 18

Exactly how the three are connected remains to be seen. However, I have never seen Lara as excited as she is today.

I find that sometimes Lara can be a bit vague or disorganized. She often seemed that way in my Grade 7 classes; neither Physical Education nor Computing Studies seemed to interest her very much. Lara is one of those students who quietly fades into the background. She doesn't make a fuss. She is not a bother. Her grades are passable but not memorable. With 30 or more students in most high school classes, it is often hard to recall students like Lara after having taught them for only one year.

My double block of Year 11 Computer Science ends and I head for the A-Block staffroom. Lara is waiting at the door with two friends.

We're here.

Let me put my books down and I will be right back.

As I enter the staffroom Silvana passes me the Year 7 Camp consent forms, Mark asks if volleyball training is on today, and Eberhard reminds me that the math teachers' meeting is on Thursday. I put my books on my desk and retrace my steps, following two math teachers, Andrew and Alfred, out the door. As I leave I hold the door open as Ms. McLure, the mathematics coordinator, quietly enters the staffroom.

Lara and her friends are waiting patiently. They follow me out of A-Block into the lower quadrangle. I am struck by the multicoloured summer outfits worn by the staff in contrast to the muted grey and blue school uniforms of the students. The colour of their uniforms reflects the parents' conservative values in this *nouveau riche* suburb on the northeastern fringes of Melbourne.

Lara, you have my undivided attention! What's this Angels thing?

It was on the Triple M last night. It's a competition. The school that collects the most Big M labels wins a free Angels concert at their school.

All three girls squeal in unison: "Yeaaaaa!" I clasp my hands over my ears.

Big M labels?

Yes. There are two on every carton.

I probably have one Big M milk drink a month (usually after yelling myself hoarse at a rock concert). I like vanilla malt. All the other flavours are too sweet (e.g., strawberry, banana, chocolate, etc.). A momentary thought passes through my mind: "Should a PE teacher be supporting a contest involving sugary drinks?"

Go on.

We can get the whole school to bring in Big Ms. And we can cut out the labels.

The thought of squeezing another activity into my already busy schedule makes me cringe.

How long is the competition? When did it start? When does it finish?

10 weeks. It started last week. It finishes on March 15th.

And you want the whole school involved?

Yes, that is the only way we will have a chance of winning.

Lara has a point. We are a mid-sized high school compared to other public schools and some of the larger private schools that have more than one campus.

Let me think on it.

Lara shakes her head in mock contempt at my use of the currently popular Meatloaf lyric. She doesn't agree with all of my musical tastes!

That night my younger brother who is possibly the biggest Angels fan in Australia (he rarely misses a concert and travels interstate to see them perform) fills me in on the details. Schools throughout Victoria have 6 weeks to collect Big M labels. There are two Big M labels on each milk carton. Each label is worth one point. The final points tally has to be verified by the school principal. The school with the most points by March 15th wins a fully-staged Angels concert at their school.

The Angels are one of the most popular, if not the most popular, bands in Australia. They perform at large venues or stadiums. It is hard to visualize an Angels concert in the East Doncaster High School gymnasium.

Lara's fantasy of winning seems just that, a fantasy. Students from our school are very successful in their academic studies, on the sports field, and in the performing arts. But are they milk-carton-collecting champions?

Lara seeks me out 45 minutes before the start of school the next day indicating her evident excitement for the project. I am knee-deep in orienteering equipment.

Mr. Clarke. Melissa and I collected some Big Ms last night.

Lara holds up a plastic Safeway bag containing a dozen or more Big M cartons.

She smiles. I smile.
She laughs. I laugh.
We both know I am being manipulated.

ANTHONY CLARKE

> *OK. Lara. I'm in. But first I have to run this by Mr. Burns.*
>
> *Where can I put these?*
>
> *Leave them with me. I will put them in the A-Block staffroom.*
>
> *Thank youuuuuuuuu, Mr. Clarke.*

It's only a small thing, but when a student says "Thank you," with such delight and enthusiasm, then you can't help but feel the influence that you, as a teacher, can have on the students in your care. Much later in my career, Gary Fenstermacher (1992) put into words what I was unable to articulate or perhaps even recognize that day: that there are two powerful forces at play in education, a "system of schooling" versus "the educative agenda." The system of schooling is about timetabling, scheduling, assessing, recording, and reporting. The educative agenda is entirely different in its emphasis: it focuses on providing support and success, in the fullest sense possible (not just academic), in the ways that students come to know and interact with the world. Unbeknown to me, I was responding to the educative agenda.

Mr. Burns, our principal, is a caring but cautious gentleman. Furthermore, every school decision he makes only occurs after he gives it serious consideration. The Big M/Triple M Angels contest won't be an easy sell. If I propose a harebrained idea, in the kindest possible way he will say "No." If I propose a fair to middling idea, in the kindest possible way he will say "No." If I have a good idea, he will say, "Can I get back to you?" He definitely won't make an on-the-spot decision.

> *Tom, thanks for seeing me. I have an idea I would like to run by you.*

He nods.

> *I am glad you are sitting down! Just joking. I was approached by Lara Diamond, in Year 10, with an idea for a school-wide event.*
>
> *I can't place her.*
>
> *She is a good kid. Nothing outstanding but solid. She wants the school to enter a contest.*
>
> *A contest?*
>
> *Yes. With Triple M.*

His left eyebrow goes up.

> *The rock station?*
>
> *Yes. We have to collect Big Ms.*

His right eyebrow joins his left.

> *The milk company?*

Yes. The prize is an Angels concert.

Both eyebrows collide with his hairline. Clearly Lara's proposal surprises him.

He pauses. After a few more questions he casts the contest in the broader context of the school community. Is the Student Representative Council involved? Will it compete with other school events? Would the staff be supportive? Etc. He doesn't say "No" but he is laying out the "bigger picture." I indicate that these are all good questions but that I don't have the answers just yet. I suggest that, if nothing else, a school-wide contest provides a good chance to build East Doncaster's *esprit de corps*—something that I know Tom will see as a positive.

To further allay his concerns I suggest that it is highly unlikely that we would actually win the contest—there are too many other schools bigger than us—and that our participation will likely peter out before the March 15th deadline. Nonetheless, we would all have had some fun along the way. Tom glances down at the papers on his desk, signalling that our conversation is drawing to a close, and asks:

Anything else that I should know?

At the end of March we could sell our Big M collection to the highest bidder!

Both eyebrows up again.

Just joking!

Eyebrows back to the neutral position. Tom's response is not unexpected.

Can I get back to you?

The fact that Tom is willing to consider the possibility of the Big M/Triple M Angels contest is a good sign.

At the end of the day I meet with Lara and four of her friends (the newly formed Angels Committee). I fill them in on my meeting with the principal and ask them how they think we should proceed if we are allowed to enter the competition. They offer a few suggestions and agree to draw up a plan. As they head for the school gate, backpacks slung over their shoulders, I wonder if any homework will get done this week.

To my surprise Lara places a plan on my desk first thing the next morning. I marvel at what she has sketched out. She seems to have left no stone unturned. Lara has a future career in event planning! I am beginning to think that I have underestimated her talents.

After recess, I catch up with Tom. He has a few more questions and with the help of Lara's plan I am able to answer most of them. He warms to the idea of the contest. He lays down "a few boundary conditions" if the school is going to be involved (e.g., a staff member overseeing the competition). After 30 minutes our conversation draws to a close, by which time Tom agrees that a school-wide event like the Big M/Triple M Angels concert would set a good tone for the start of the school year. He gives his approval to enter the competition believing that our chances of winning are slim to nil.

ANTHONY CLARKE

THE COMPETITION

Monday, Week 2 of the competition

With the principal's approval, Lara and her team swing into action. The Angels Committee commandeers one of the art prep rooms and begins making badges and posters. They place announcements in the daily bulletin and co-opt two other teachers, Mr. Tomsett (Mark) and Miss Criveli (Silvana), to help with the logistics.

Mr. Burns makes an official announcement over the public address system on Tuesday morning and cheers can be heard from classrooms around the school. On Thursday the students start dropping off Big M cartons at the A-Block staffroom.

By Friday the aroma of stale milk is overpowering and we shift the operation to the school garage in the lower quadrangle. We now have a larger space to wash and bundle the Big M labels.

By week's end, our tally reaches 4,125 labels. Not too bad for a school of 1,000 students.

Week 3 of the competition

Lara and her friends continue to promote the competition (e.g., by visiting and speaking to students in classrooms throughout the school). Mark and Silvana take responsibility for the garage and enrol a small team of volunteers to assist (mostly Grade 9 and 10 students).

A noticeable pattern to the Big M contribution begins to emerge. The senior students seem to decide that it is "uncool" to be associated with a Year 10 project even if they are Angels fans. At the other end of the grade-level spectrum, the Year 7 and 8 students are curious but their musical tastes haven't as yet fully embraced the type of loud, rock and roll music that characterizes the Angels hits.

The few junior and senior students who are enthusiastic drop off their Big M cartons either before or after school when there aren't too many students around to see them doing so. Despite the Angels Committee's attempt at school-wide participation, the project is largely perceived as a Grade 9 and 10 effort.

Some schools in the competition ring in their weekly tallies to Triple M who announce the leading contenders each Saturday at 7:05 pm, directly after the news broadcast. As expected, the bigger public and private schools are reporting large tallies. Geelong Grammar leads with over 12,000 labels.

Our tally: 7,461.

Week 4 of the competition

Lara has redoubled her efforts. She seems to be everywhere as the spokesperson for EDHS's efforts: leading by example (collecting and contributing Big Ms); encouraging and supporting the Angels Committee in their daily work; and helping out in the garage during lunchtime and after school.

It is clear that she and her fellow supporters are scrounging milk cartons from wherever they can find them; some contributions are very old and battered. Lara's enthusiasm never seems to dim. Unfortunately the accumulation of our Big M cartons doesn't match her enthusiasm. After all, how much milk can Year 9 and 10 students drink?

Tom is delighted overall with our attempt to involve the school community and mentions on more than one occasion that "*it's the journey, not the destination, that is important*," a refrain that will no doubt appear in an upcoming "Newsletter to Parents."

It's 5:30 pm, Friday afternoon, and Mark, Silvana, and I are the last ones in the garage. The students have all left. We have just finished the weekly count: 12,932 labels. I think that the students were anticipating that our tally would be much larger. Unfortunately, it barely matches the tallies of the leading schools reported by Triple M last Friday.

Nonetheless, we look with pride at the four neatly stacked boxes of labels in the garage and know that Lara and her committee can be well satisfied that they have done their best. Silvana locks the garage and we head home.

On the weekend I catch up on school work that the Big M competition has interrupted during the past week and forget about the competition.

My brother calls at 7:06 pm on Saturday night.

Congratulations!

What for?

Triple M just announced your tally. You're in front with 20,000 points. Geelong Grammar School is in second place with 19,000.

What? We only have 13,000 labels.

That's not what Triple M says. You are in the lead.

Are you sure it wasn't Doncaster High School just down the road?

Nope. It is East Donnie for sure.

I'm confused.

Week 5 of the competition

The school is abuzz on Monday morning. It seems as if everyone has heard that we are in the lead. As I look across the quadrangle, a steady flow of students are leaving plastic bags of Big Ms at the garage. Even junior and senior students are dropping off their contributions right up to the start of the school day.

I wave to Silvana and Mark and join them at the garage. We marvel at the small mountain of Big Ms cartons before us; at least as many again as we had collected up to this point last Friday. The garage volunteers will have their work cut out this week.

As we ponder the difference between our Friday night tally and Triple M's Saturday night announcement a yell from across the quadrangle catches our attention.

Mr. Clarke! Mr. Tomsett! Miss Crivelli!

The bell for the first class sounds as Lara jogs our way. She has a big grin on her face and a plastic bag of Big Ms in each hand.

Lara!

Morning Mr. Clarke.

Lara?

Two Grade 7s gave me these.

She places the bags on the garage floor. In response, I choose my words carefully.

They will add nicely to our lead position in the competition.

Before I have a chance to say any more, she blurts out:

O.K. Sorry. It was me. I rang Triple M.

You did?

And they asked me for an estimate. I am not very good at estimating. Mr. Tomsett can tell you that (Mark is Lara's math teacher).

She can see the disappointment in our faces as Mark points out the discrepancy between our Friday night tally and Lara's Saturday night estimate.

Lara, we don't have 20,000 labels.

She glances at the new pile of Big Ms in the centre of the garage floor.

We might have now?

Lara's cheeks turn red signalling that she recognizes she is being chastised. We look at each other as we consider our predicament. I make a decision.

OK. That might be true but we have to think about Triple M's announcement. Let's see what we have by the end of this week and if we fall short of 20,000 we will ring Triple M and tell them the truth.

We all nod in agreement. Before Lara leaves Silvana has some advice.

Lara, please, please, please, no more ringing Triple M without checking with us?

OK. Miss Crivelli. No more phone calls.

The bell rings for the start of the school day as we head off to our various classes.

Despite the circumstances leading to Triple M's announcement that we are leading the competition, it is clear that our Monday morning's contributions mark a turning point in the school community's response to the Big M/Triple M Angels contest. Big Ms continue to flow in over the course of the week, at times overwhelming the garage volunteers who struggle to keep up with washing, cutting, counting, and bundling the labels.

At Friday lunchtime, Lara, the Angels Committee, Silvana, Mark, and I meet in the garage. Our tally at the moment is 21,567. We still have more Big Ms that need to be cut and counted. We decide not to ring Triple M.

Instead, Lara suggests that we ask the principal to make an announcement at the end of the school day letting the students know our current tally. Tom agrees and when he makes the announcement, resounding cheers can be heard from around the school.

Triple M's announcement on Saturday night indicates that we are neck and neck with Geelong Grammar School for first place and that Marcellin College is close behind.

Week 6 of the competition

The school has gone nuts!

Year 12 students are spotted dumpster diving at the local mall for Big M cartons; parents are dropping off Big M cartons during the day; and even Mr. Burns is seen dropping a few cartons in the Big M collection box in the main staffroom. The school is totally transformed. Silvana, Mark, and I call it the "Lara Effect."

I am beginning to see Lara differently from the student who stopped me in the quadrangle and asked about entering the Angels contest five weeks ago. My earlier estimation of Lara's talents has been challenged dramatically in the past few weeks. The impact that she has had on the school is nothing short of extraordinary. Even Mr. Burns is amazed by the palpable sense of pride, excitement, and anticipation that Lara's idea and her enthusiasm for the project has created across the school community.

Also I have begun to think differently about how and in what way our schools serve our students. I am a strong believer in "success breeds success." And unquestionably Lara has been extraordinarily successful in ways that aren't measured on end-of-year exams. For a school that prides itself on student achievement, Lara is challenging us to think more broadly about curriculum. Years later, I realize more fully the broader implications of the educative agenda and how teachers are called upon to act in their daily practice with students (Wrigley, Lingard, & Thomson, 2012).

On the final Friday afternoon, we tie the last few bundles together and calculate our tally. Tom Burns signs the official letter and we fax it off to Triple M. The office phone rings 30 minutes later with Triple M requesting confirmation from our principal of the total. Mr. Burns obliges.

At 7:05 pm on Saturday night, Triple M announces the results of the contest. They work their way from third place to first place.

And in first place, with 35,854 points, the winning school: East Doncaster High School.

ANTHONY CLARKE

Three months later

The Angels perform live at East Doncaster High School.

Figure 19

WHAT LARA TAUGHT ME

Within the context of *Speaking of Learning,* I have tried to illustrate the learning that took place when I began to articulate for myself the difference between what it meant to be a *teacher* and what it meant to be an *educator*. Put simply, I began to realize that, above all, my responsibility to my students was to facilitate (and model) how "to live well in the world." The full realization of this concept did not occur in a single "Aha" moment but was the result of numerous encounters with students, parents, and staff over the years at East Doncaster High School where I taught for 12 years.

My engagement with Lara was perhaps one of the most significant events leading to this realization. The scale and magnitude of what Lara achieved was the tipping point as my view of schooling, its purpose, and its potential shifted significantly. Others have written about this notion more eloquently (e.g., Palmer, 1997) but it took the immediacy of my experience with Lara in the context of my daily practice (Munby & Russell, 1994) for me to fully appreciate schooling and curriculum in its broadest context (Pinar, Reynolds, Slattery, & Taubman, 1995).

What if I had said "No" to Lara?

Supporting students' requests to participate in deviant non-curricular events was not a part of my teacher preparation. Melbourne University prepared me and the Victorian Ministry of Education employed me to teach physical education, mathematics, and computer science. Based on the explicit and implicit messages conveyed to me as part of my teacher education program, as a high school teacher my task was to prepare students for their Year 12 examinations. I think that missing from both my preparation and initial employment was any sense of the moral and ethical purposes of schooling that were, much later, to have a profound effect on my understanding of what I did in schools (precipitated by events such as my work with Lara detailed above). Maybe these elements were present in my teacher education program or the early days of my career and I just didn't recognize them.

If as Southern suggests, "[a]s relational beings, we construct our world through language," (Southern, 2005, p. 39) then the difference between being a teacher and an educator takes on particular significance in this context. At East Doncaster High School I taught three subjects. I now realize that that duty occupied only 50% of what I did at EDHS. Lara helped me to understand what constituted the other 50%.

As I reflect on my current role as a teacher educator preparing young people for the profession, I wonder if the speed with which I was prepared, and at which we currently prepare young people for teaching, means that there is a stronger likelihood that the essence of being an educator is in danger of being lost altogether. We have many wonderful young people entering the profession but in my recent experience a number of those beginners quickly retreat and hold fast to very traditional and conservative ways of teaching and seem to stay that way.

My story then is a cautionary tale of why and how the difference between being a teacher and being an educator is not something that should be taken for granted nor should it be left to fate or chance; the difference and the importance it has for the students in our classrooms should be uppermost in our minds.

In telling Lara's story, I am reminded that:

> I identify, problematize, and specify what it is that I am being attentive to. As I do this, I also draw on my feelings and emotions in re-storying the event. I set the stage and paint the landscape to sufficiently portray as vividly as possible the essence of the event as it unfolded for me. I give emphasis to some elements and relegate others to background colour. Each of these decisions requires that I pause, think, and then act—that is, to make choices.
> ... Unavoidably, I am deeply implicated in the retelling. The story and "I" are interwoven and although the difference between the two might not be readily apparent ... the rendering of 'the other' is a always a rendering of 'self.' (Clarke, 2012, p. 61)

So, although this story is about Lara, more importantly it is about what Lara taught me. It is a lesson about the broader purposes of schooling. It is a lesson about the difference between being a teacher and being an educator. And it represents what I currently try to live in my daily practice with students, teachers, and teacher educators in the hope that they will reap the rewards of their efforts, whatever form those rewards might take. For example, one of the most delightful moments in the Lara story happened immediately after the concert. Doc Neeson, the lead singer of the Angels, asked to meet the students who had been responsible for EDHS winning the contest. As a result, not only did Lara get to meet her rock and roll hero but had her photograph taken (with her blond hair somewhat dishevelled after the concert) standing proudly beside him. What a thrill!

Figure 20

REFERENCES

Clarke, A. (2012). Burgeo and back! Living pedagogically: Catching oneself in the act of being attentive to pedagogy. In A. Cohen, M. Porath, A. Clarke, H. Bai, C. Leggo, & K. Meyer, *Speaking of teaching: Inclinations, inspirations, and innerworkings* (pp. 55–62). Rotterdam, The Netherlands: Sense.

Fenstermacher, G. (1992). *Policy development and teacher education: An educative agenda vs. a system of schooling*. Invited presentation, University of British Columbia, Vancouver, BC.

Munby, H., & Russell, T. (1994). The authority of experience in learning to teach: Messages from a physics methods class. *Journal of Teacher Education, 45*(2), 86–95.

Palmer. P. (1997). *The courage to teach*. San Francisco, CA: Jossey-Bass.

Pinar, W., Reynolds, W., Slattery, P., & Taubman, P. (1995). *Understanding curriculum*. New York, NY: Peter Lang.

Southern, N. (2005). Creating cultures of collaboration that thrive on diversity: A transformational perspective on building collaborative capital. In M. M. Beyerlein, S. T. Beyerlein, & F. A. Kennedy (Eds.), *Collaborative capital: Creating in-tangible value: Vol. 2. Advances in Interdisciplinary Studies of Work Teams* (pp. 33–72). San Diego, CA: Elsevier.

Wrigley, T., Lingard, B., & Thomson, P. (2012) Pedagogies of transformation: Keeping hope alive in troubled times. *Critical Studies in Education, 53*(1), 95–108.

HAVING SPOKEN OF LEARNING

Recollections, Revelations, and Realizations

Not surprisingly, we have learned much from being members of our group. Our group has met on an ongoing basis since 2006; a rather long life for an academic group. As well, the group has emphasized the development of its culture and cohesiveness, and in particular, the sharing of the personal and human dimension of each of us has formed the container within which the two book projects have emerged. Our research is based in personal narratives and the intent is to convey what matters to each of us about learning and what has formed us as human beings who are also learners and educators.

In the preceding chapters we have *recollected* experiences, shared our *revelations*, and described our broader *realizations*.

THE LAST WORD

What lies within these pages is our collective contribution to understandings about learning and how these are integrally connected to personal life history, experience, and their imprints within the educator. Our hope is that you, the readers, will be inspired to look more deeply into your own life experiences and inner and intersubjective worlds in the service of becoming increasingly the educators and models of learning that we all would like to have and to have had.

ABOUT THE AUTHORS OF SPEAKING OF LEARNING

Avraham Cohen: I don't know that I have ever had a firm sense of identity; rather what has come to be an increasingly fluid one. I have made a virtue out of what used to trouble me. Perhaps this explains my affinity for Eastern philosophy and practices, particularly the ideas of *anatta,* no fixed self, and *sunyata,* emptiness; an emptiness that denotes potential. I continue to grow, learn, and be amused and bemused. I hope it will continue forever thus. And as a Daoist immortal "forever" is, of course, a distinct possibility.

***

Heesoon Bai: Throughout my life, I have learned to take on many roles: a little girl running around amusing elders and being amused herself; a budding teenage existential philosopher; a serious, tireless, studious student; a companion, caregiver, and nurse to my mother; a mother whose identity seems far more than a role; a servant leader both at home and at school; a sedulous wife and homemaker; and a philosopher-teacher whose calling continues to inspire, intrigue, and animate her.

***

Carl Leggo: I am a papa, poet, and professor who has spent his long life in love with learning, always yearning for learning, not always thinking about earning a living, but always listening attentively with the ear at the heart of all learning, still convinced in my 60th year that being a learner is inextricably connected to learning to be.

***

Marion Porath: I have been a learner all my life, in and out of school. I have learned in many ways and studied and researched learning. Now, in retirement, learning takes a different turn—more personal, more artistic, more introspective, more free, and more joyful than ever.

***

Karen Meyer: For myself I want nothing more than to be a good writer, teacher, citizen, partner, mother, grandmother, daughter, and friend. For the world I want much more—peace, justice, sustainability, and consideration of children's rights and well-being in global and community decisions.

***

Anthony Clarke: Still doing cartwheels.

***

CPSIA information can be obtained at www.ICGtesting.com
Printed in the USA
LVOW05s0815220814

400135LV00001B/1/P